SEIZE THE KEYS OF THE TOEIC® L&R TEST

Masako Yasumaru   Akiko Watanabe   Noriko Sunagawa
Akiko Takamori   Yasushi Totoki   Andrew Zitzmann

JN125956

KINSEIDO

Kinseido Publishing Co., Ltd.

3-21 Kanda Jimbo-cho, Chiyoda-ku,
Tokyo 101-0051, Japan

First published 2020 by Kinseido Publishing Co., Ltd.

Cover design Nampoosha Co., Ltd.
Text design   Asahi Media International Inc.

 音声ファイル無料ダウンロード

http://www.kinsei-do.co.jp/download/4110

この教科書で 🎧 DL 00 の表示がある箇所の音声は、上記 URL または QR コードにて
無料でダウンロードできます。自習用音声としてご活用ください。

- ▶ PC からのダウンロードをお勧めします。スマートフォンなどでダウンロードされる場合は、
  ダウンロード前に「解凍アプリ」をインストールしてください。
- ▶ URL は、**検索ボックスではなくアドレスバー (URL 表示欄)** に入力してください。
- ▶ お使いのネットワーク環境によっては、ダウンロードできない場合があります。

🔘 **CD 00** 左記の表示がある箇所の音声は、教室用 CD（Class Audio CD）に収録されています。

本テキストの特徴とその使い方

　グローバル人材の育成と確保が求められる中で、ますます多くの企業が、英語力を計る目安や採用・昇進の判断材料として *TOEIC*® Listening & Reading Test（以下 *TOEIC*® L&R）を利用しています。また近年では、*TOEIC*® L&R のスコアをレベル判定や成績評価に用いたり、大学院の進学要件としたり、合否判定の優遇措置としたりするケースも増えてきています。

　このように *TOEIC*® L&R の需要が高まる中、高いスコアを取得するためにはどうすればよいのでしょうか。地道な努力を重ねることが必要なのは言うまでもありませんが、それに加えて、全体の構成・分量・時間配分などを把握し、ビジネス関連の語彙や表現、そして *TOEIC*® L&R のテスト形式そのものに慣れることも重要です。しかしながら、ただひたすら問題を解いて頻出の出題パターンと自分の弱点を攻略するというのは、なかなか大変な作業です。

　そこで、*TOEIC*® L&R を熟知した著者陣による問題の徹底分析に基づいて作成された「超実践 *TOEIC*® L&R 攻略テキスト」が、この ***SEIZE THE KEYS OF THE TOEIC*® *L&R TEST*** です。以下にその特徴と使い方をまとめていますので、うまく使いこなし、ぜひともスコアアップに役立ててください。

①「内容に関するテーマ」とKey Vocabulary

　各ユニットに、*TOEIC*® L&R で頻出の場面を想定した「内容に関するテーマ」を設定しています。また、巻末には、そのテーマ特有の頻出語句を集めたKey Vocabulary が収録されています。本テキストの問題は、このKey Vocabulary の語句を繰り返し用いながら「内容に関するテーマ」に沿って作成されていますので、問題を解き進めるうちに、頻出の場面設定と頻出語句を自然に学ぶことができます。Key Vocabulary はとにかく実戦を意識して作成していますので、しっかり覚えて身に付ければ、教科書や授業内容の理解に大いに役立つだけでなく、実際のスコアアップにかなりの効果が期待できます。

②習得すべき頻出「文法テーマ」

　各ユニットには「内容に関するテーマ」と並行して、習得すべき頻出「文法テーマ」を設定しています。文法は、ただ問題をやみくもに解くよりも、テーマごとに知識を整理しながら、出題傾向に合わせて練習するのが最も効果的です。中学・高校で学んだ文法事項を復習しながら、*TOEIC*® L&R 頻出の文法ポイントを効率よく押さえていきましょう。

③「ターゲット」と「解法のポイント」

　全てのパートに、*TOEIC*® L&R の問題パターンを意識した「ターゲット」と「解法のポイント」を設定し、「*TOEIC*® L&R に慣れるための鍵」を分かりやすく解説しています。「ターゲット」では *TOEIC*® L&R 独特の出題パターンについて紹介し、「解法のポイント」では具体的なアドバイスが提示されています。それぞれのパートの頻出パターン、解答者が陥りやすい間違いなど、スコアアップに役立つヒントがぎっしり詰まっています。同じ間違いを繰り返しながら、やみくもに問題を解き進めていくのではなく、それらのヒントをしっかり生かして、効率的にスコアアップを狙いましょう。

④音声データのダウンロード

　本テキストの音声データはダウンロードして入手することができます（Introductionと Review Testを除く）。それらを最大限に活用すれば、リスニング用の問題集を買う必要はありません。音声をスマートフォンや音楽デバイスなどにダウンロードして、毎日1ユニットずつ聞きましょう。音声のスピードが、実際の *TOEIC*® L&Rよりも若干遅めに設定されていますので、耳を慣らす練習にはうってつけです。授業の予習・復習に役立つのはもちろんのこと、頻出語句の正しい発音や英語独特のイントネーションを浴びて耳を鍛えることで、本番での確実なスコアアップが期待できます。

⑤Review Test［復習テスト］

　本テキストは、前半ユニット（Unit 1 ~ Unit 6）の復習用としてReview Test 1を、また後半ユニット（Unit 7 ~ Unit 12）の復習用としてReview Test 2を用意しています。これらのReview Testは、対象範囲の学習内容が着実に身に付いているかを確認するための復習応用問題です。このテストで好成績を上げるためには、各ユニットを学習する際にただ答えを暗記するのではなく、その答えに至る過程と理由をきちんと理解することが大切です。前半・後半それぞれの復習を行って、本物の実力を付けましょう。巻末にはReview Test用の切り取り式解答用マークシートも用意しています。

⑥全体の構成

　1回（90分）の授業で取り組めるよう、各ユニットにつき4つのパートを取りあげ、バランス良くコンパクトに構成されています。Part 1, Part 7は全てのユニットで、Part 2, Part 3, Part 4はそれぞれ3ユニットに一度、Part 5はUnit 2・6・8・12を除く全てのユニットで、Part 6はUnit 2・6・8・12でそれぞれ扱っています。詳しくは、Contentsを参照してください。

　最後に、本テキストの刊行にあたり、前作に引き続き金星堂の皆様には大変お世話になりました。この場を借りてお礼申し上げます。

著者一同

本書は CheckLink（チェックリンク）対応テキストです。

CheckLinkのアイコンが表示されている設問は、CheckLink に対応しています。

CheckLink を使用しなくても従来通りの授業ができますが、特色をご理解いただき、授業活性化のためにぜひご活用ください。

CheckLinkの特色について

　大掛かりで複雑な従来のe-learningシステムとは異なり、CheckLink のシステムは大きな特色として次の3点が挙げられます。

1．これまで行われてきた教科書を使った授業展開に大幅な変化を加えることなく、専門的な知識なしにデジタル学習環境を導入することができる。
2．PC教室やCALL教室といった最新の機器が導入された教室に限定されることなく、普通教室を使用した授業でもデジタル学習環境を導入することができる。
3．授業中での使用に特化し、教師・学習者双方のモチベーション・集中力をアップさせ、授業自体を活性化することができる。

▶教科書を使用した授業に「デジタル学習環境」を導入できる

　本システムでは、学習者は教科書のCheckLinkのアイコンが表示されている設問にPCやスマートフォン、携帯電話端末からインターネットを通して解答します。そして教師は、授業中にリアルタイムで解答結果を把握し、正解率などに応じて有効な解説を行うことができるようになっています。教科書自体は従来と何ら変わりはありません。解答の手段としてCheckLinkを使用しない場合でも、従来通りの教科書として使用して授業を行うことも、もちろん可能です。

▶教室環境を選ばない

　従来の多機能なe-learning教材のように学習者側の画面に多くの機能を持たせることはせず、「解答する」ことに機能を特化しました。PCだけでなく、一部タブレット端末やスマートフォン、携帯電話端末からの解答も可能です。したがって、PC教室やCALL教室といった大掛かりな教室は必要としません。普通教室でもCheckLinkを用いた授業が可能です。教師はPCだけでなく、一部タブレット端末やスマートフォンからも解答結果の確認をすることができます。

▶授業を活性化するための支援システム

　本システムは予習や復習のツールとしてではなく、授業中に活用されることで真価を発揮する仕組みになっています。CheckLink というデジタル学習環境を通じ、教師と学習者双方が授業中に解答状況などの様々な情報を共有することで、学習者はやる気を持って解答し、教師は解答状況に応じて効果的な解説を行う、という好循環を生み出します。CheckLinkは、普段の授業をより活力のあるものへと変えていきます。

　上記3つの大きな特色以外にも、掲示板などの授業中に活用できる機能を用意しています。従来通りの教科書としても使用はできますが、ぜひCheckLinkの機能をご理解いただき、普段の授業をより活性化されたものにしていくためにご活用ください。

CheckLink の使い方

CheckLink は、PC や一部タブレット端末、スマートフォン、携帯電話端末を用いて、この教科書の ↻CheckLink のアイコン表示のある設問に解答するシステムです。

・初めて CheckLink を使う場合、以下の要領で**「学習者登録」**と**「教科書登録」**を行います。
・一度登録を済ませれば、あとは毎回**「ログイン画面」**から入るだけです。CheckLink を使う教科書が増えたときだけ、改めて**「教科書登録」**を行ってください。

CheckLink URL

https://checklink.kinsei-do.co.jp/student/

QR コードの読み取りができる端末の場合はこちらから ▶ ▶ ▶

ご注意ください！ 上記 URL は**「検索ボックス」**でなく**「アドレスバー (URL 表示欄)」**に入力してください。

▶学習者登録

①上記 URL にアクセスすると、右のページが表示されます。学校名を入力し「ログイン画面へ」をクリックしてください。
PC の場合は「PC 用はこちら」をクリックして PC 用ページを表示します。同様に学校名を入力し「ログイン画面へ」をクリックしてください。

②ログイン画面が表示されたら**「初めての方はこちら」**をクリックし「学習者登録画面」に入ります。

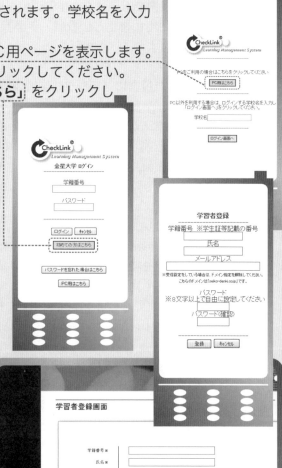

③自分の学籍番号、氏名、メールアドレス（学校のメールなど **PC メールを推奨**）を入力し、次に**任意のパスワード**を 8 桁以上 20 桁未満（半角英数字）で入力します。なお、学籍番号はパスワードとして使用することはできません。

④「パスワード確認」は、❸で入力したパスワードと同じものを入力します。

⑤最後に「登録」ボタンをクリックして登録は完了です。次回からは、「ログイン画面」から学籍番号とパスワードを入力してログインしてください。

▶教科書登録

①ログイン後、メニュー画面から「教科書登録」を選び（PCの場合はその後「新規登録」ボタンをクリック）、「教科書登録」画面を開きます。

②教科書と受講する授業を登録します。
教科書の最終ページにある、**教科書固有番号**のシールをはがし、印字された**16桁の数字とアルファベット**を入力します。

③授業を担当される先生から連絡された**11桁の授業ID**を入力します。

④最後に「登録」ボタンをクリックして登録は完了です。

⑤実際に使用する際は「教科書一覧」（PCの場合は「教科書選択画面」）の該当する教科書名をクリックすると、「問題解答」の画面が表示されます。

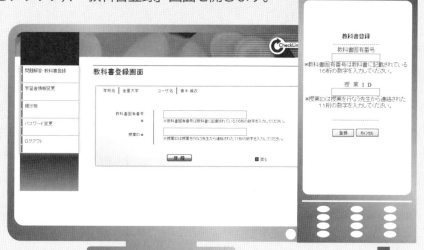

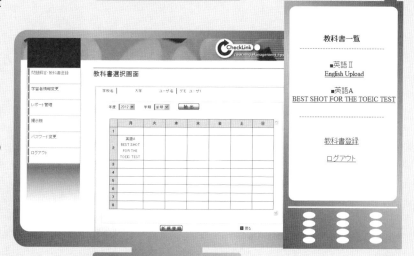

▶問題解答

①問題は教科書を見ながら解答します。この教科書の **CheckLink** のアイコン表示のある設問に解答できます。

②問題が表示されたら選択肢を選びます。

③表示されている問題に解答した後、「解答」ボタンをクリックすると解答が登録されます。

▶CheckLink 推奨環境

PC

推奨 OS
  Windows 7, 10 以降
  MacOS X 以降

推奨ブラウザ
  Internet Explorer 8.0 以上
  Firefox 40.0 以上
  Google Chrome 50 以上
  Safari

携帯電話・スマートフォン
  3G 以降の携帯電話（docomo, au, softbank）
  iPhone, iPad（iOS9 〜）
  Android OS スマートフォン、タブレット

・最新の推奨環境についてはウェブサイトをご確認ください。
・上記の推奨環境を満たしている場合でも、機種によってはご利用いただけない場合もあります。また、推奨環境は技術動向等により変更される場合があります。

▶CheckLink 開発
CheckLink は奥田裕司 福岡大学教授、正興 IT ソリューション株式会社、株式会社金星堂によって共同開発されました。

CheckLink は株式会社金星堂の登録商標です。

CheckLink の使い方に関するお問い合わせは…

正興ITソリューション株式会社　CheckLink 係

e-mail checklink@seiko-denki.co.jp

Contents

SEIZE THE KEYS OF THE TOEIC® L&R TEST

TOEIC® Listening & Reading Testについて

TOEIC® Listening & Reading Test（以下 *TOEIC*® L&R）は、オフィスや日常生活でのコミュニケーションの場面における英語のリスニング力とリーディング力を測るテストです。リスニングとリーディングの2つのセクションで構成されています。

Section	Part	問題形式	問題数
Listening （約45分）	1	**Photographs（写真描写問題）** • 1枚の写真につき4つの短い説明文を聞いて、最も適切に写真を描写しているものを選ぶ。 • 説明文は印刷されていない。	6
	2	**Question-Response（応答問題）** • 1つの質問または発言と3つの応答を聞いて、最も適切な応答を選ぶ。 • 質問または発言、応答は印刷されていない。	25
	3	**Conversations（会話問題）** • 2人または3人による会話と設問を聞いて、4つの選択肢から最も適切なものを選ぶ。 • 会話は印刷されていない。	39 ［1つの会話に3設問 ×13セット］
	4	**Talks（説明文問題）** • 説明文と設問を聞いて、4つの選択肢から最も適切なものを選ぶ。 • 説明文は印刷されていない。	30 ［1つの説明文に3設問 ×10セット］
Reading （75分）	5	**Incomplete Sentences（短文穴埋め問題）** • 短い文の中にある空所に入る語（句）として最も適切なものを、4つの選択肢から選ぶ。	30
	6	**Text Completion（長文穴埋め問題）** • 文書の中にある4つの空所それぞれにつき、4つの選択肢から最も適切な語（句）や文を選ぶ。	16 ［1つの文書に4設問 ×4セット］
	7	**Single passages（1つの文書）** • 1つの文書と設問を読み、4つの選択肢から最も適切なものを選ぶ。 **Multiple passages（複数の文書）** • 2～3つの関連する文書と設問を読み、4つの選択肢から最も適切なものを選ぶ。	**Single passages：29** ［1つの文書に2～4設問 ×10セット］ **Multiple passages：25** ［2～3つの文書に5設問 ×5セット］

- マークシート方式のテストで、問題は全て英語で構成されています。
- スコアは、リスニングセクションとリーディングセクションそれぞれ5～495点、計10～990点で評価されます。
- リスニングセクションの音声は、アメリカ、イギリス、カナダ、オーストラリアの発音です。

Sample Questions

Introductionを始める前に、Part 1 ～ 7の問題形式について詳しく確認しましょう。

Listening Section

■ Part 1 Photographs （写真描写問題）

1枚の写真につき (A) ～ (D)の4つの短い説明文を聞いて、最も適切に写真の内容を描写しているものを選びます。説明文は問題用紙に印刷されていません。また、音声は一度しか放送されません。

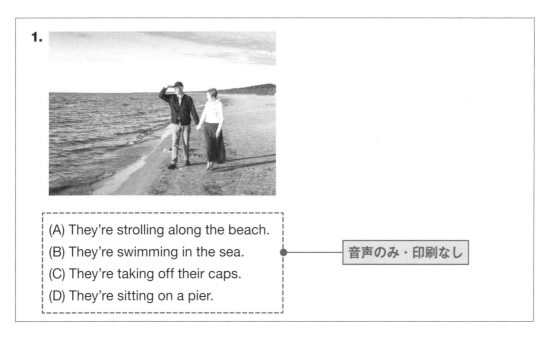

1.

(A) They're strolling along the beach.
(B) They're swimming in the sea.
(C) They're taking off their caps.
(D) They're sitting on a pier.

音声のみ・印刷なし

■ Part 2 Question-Response （応答問題）

1つの質問または発言と (A) ～ (C)の3つの応答を聞いて、最も適切な応答を選びます。質問または発言、応答は問題用紙に印刷されていません。また、音声は一度しか放送されません。

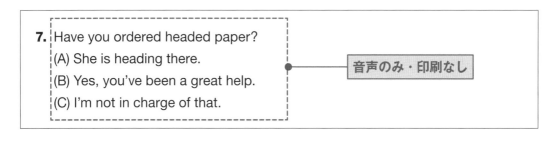

7. Have you ordered headed paper?
(A) She is heading there.
(B) Yes, you've been a great help.
(C) I'm not in charge of that.

音声のみ・印刷なし

■ Part 3 Conversations (会話問題)

2人または3人による会話と3つの設問を聞いて、それぞれの設問の(A)～(D)の4つの選択肢から最も適切なものを選びます。発言が短くてやりとりが多い会話や、elisions（音の省略）やfragments（不完全な文）が含まれる会話があります。話し手が暗示する意図を問う設問や、図表などを見て答える設問も出題されます。会話は問題用紙に印刷されていませんが、設問と選択肢は印刷されています。設問は放送されますが、選択肢は放送されません。また、音声は一度しか放送されません。

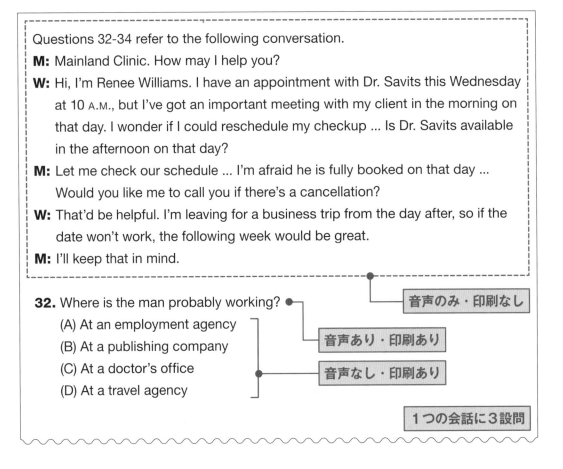

Questions 32-34 refer to the following conversation.

M: Mainland Clinic. How may I help you?

W: Hi, I'm Renee Williams. I have an appointment with Dr. Savits this Wednesday at 10 A.M., but I've got an important meeting with my client in the morning on that day. I wonder if I could reschedule my checkup ... Is Dr. Savits available in the afternoon on that day?

M: Let me check our schedule ... I'm afraid he is fully booked on that day ... Would you like me to call you if there's a cancellation?

W: That'd be helpful. I'm leaving for a business trip from the day after, so if the date won't work, the following week would be great.

M: I'll keep that in mind.

32. Where is the man probably working?
(A) At an employment agency
(B) At a publishing company
(C) At a doctor's office
(D) At a travel agency

音声のみ・印刷なし

音声あり・印刷あり

音声なし・印刷あり

1つの会話に3設問

■ Part 4 Talks (説明文問題)

説明文と3つの設問を聞いて、それぞれの設問の (A) ～ (D) の4つの選択肢から最も適切なものを選びます。話し手が暗示する意図を問う設問や、図表などを見て答える設問が出題されます。説明文は問題用紙に印刷されていませんが、設問と選択肢は印刷されています。設問は放送されますが、選択肢は放送されません。また、音声は一度しか放送されません。

Questions 95-97 refer to the following announcement and floor map.

M: Welcome to Simon's, shoppers. We offer you the freshest vegetables, fruits, meat, and many other products from our local suppliers. Along with our affordable pricing, you'll find real bargains every day! Don't forget to check out the red tags in every aisle. Would you like to save even more? Be sure to join our rewards club. You can earn reward points that can be used like cash in our store! For more details, please ask our friendly staff at the customer service counter, which is right in front of the checkout counters, on the right to the entrance. If you join today, we'll offer you a free eco-bag!

音声のみ・印刷なし

Floor Map

Area 1	Area 2	Area 3
Checkout Counters		
Area 4		

95. Who most likely are the listeners? 音声あり・印刷あり

(A) Customers at a supermarket

(B) Tellers at a financial agency

(C) Employees at a food manufacturer 音声なし・印刷あり

(D) Staff at a sports club

96. Look at the graphic. Where are the listeners 音声あり・印刷あり

interested in the rewards club advised to go?

(A) Area 1

(B) Area 2 音声なし・印刷あり

(C) Area 3

(D) Area 4

1つの説明文に3設問

13

Reading Section

■ Part 5 Incomplete Sentences（短文穴埋め問題）

短い文の中にある空所に入る語（句）として最も適切なものを、(A) ～ (D) の４つの選択肢から選びます。

---

101. I saw him ------- in the conference last summer.

    (A) participates

    (B) participating

    (C) participated

    (D) to participate

■ Part 6 Text Completion（長文穴埋め問題）

長文の中にある４つの空所それぞれにつき、(A) ～ (D) の４つの選択肢から最も適切な語（句）や文を選びます。

Questions 131-134 refer to the following e-mail.

To: All employees
From: General Affairs Department
Date: October 18
Subject: Temporary closure of main parking lot

This is to inform you that the employee parking lot ------- temporarily during the
                                    131.
week of November 4. This closure is due to the improvement work being

conducted there. Other parking lots on the premises will be open, but all

employees are advised to commute by public transportation because of limited

parking.

131. (A) closed

    (B) will be closed

    (C) have been closed

    (D) to close

１つの文書に４設問

■ Part 7 Single passages（1つの文書）・Multiple passages（複数の文書）

1つの文書、または2～3つの関連する文書と設問を読み、(A)～(D)の4つの選択肢から最も適切なものを選びます。複数名がやりとりするオンラインチャット、記事、Eメールなど、文書の種類と形式は様々です。書き手が暗示する意図を問う設問や、新たな一文を挿入するのに最も適切な箇所を選ぶ設問が出題されます。

Questions 147-148 refer to the following form.

Evergreen Home Decor
Monogramming Service Receipt

Store Location: Philadelphia   **Staff:** Maia

Date of order: 22 February, Friday

Date of pickup: 2 March, Saturday   **Time of pickup:** 3 A.M. /(P.M.)

Note: Monogrammed products can only be picked up at the store you made the order, not other locations.

Customer Information

Name: Lily Williams   **Phone:** 3263-3828

E-mail: lilywilliams@homemail.com

Monogramming Information

Item: original wool throw (white)   **Quantity:** 1

Font: script   **Text:** Sachiko   **Color:** ocean blue

Price (without tax): $8.00

Note: All sales are final.

---

147. When will the customer probably go to the store next?

(A) 22 February

(B) 1 March

(C) 2 March

(D) 3 March

148. What is indicated about Evergreen Home Decor?

(A) It is only open on weekdays.

(B) It has only one location.

(C) It does not produce original merchandise.

(D) It does not accept returns.

> 1つの文書に2～4設問
> 2～3つの文書に5設問

Introduction

Part 1

Look at the picture and choose the statement that best describes what you see in the picture.

1.

(A) (B) (C) (D)

2.

(A) (B) (C) (D)

CheckLink CD 1-03

Part 2

Listen to the question or statement and the three responses. Then choose the best response to each question or statement.

3. (A) (B) (C)

4. (A) (B) (C)

CheckLink CD 1-04

Part 3

Listen to the conversation and choose the best answer to each question.

5. What are the speakers talking about?

(A) Which vegetarian restaurant to go to

(B) How to hold a farewell party

(C) Where to buy a present

(D) What kind of beverage to bring

6. Where is the conversation taking place?

(A) At a restaurant

(B) At a vegetarian market

(C) At a company office

(D) At a catering company

7. What will the man probably do next?

(A) Make a call to Mr. Anderson

(B) Plan a company picnic

(C) Buy vegan food for his colleagues

(D) Contact a catering company

Part 4

Listen to the short talk and choose the best answer to each question.

8. What is the purpose of the call?
(A) To reschedule an appointment
(B) To respond to a complaint
(C) To ask about a contract
(D) To apologize for damage

9. What does the speaker ask the listener to do after hearing the message?
(A) Sign the document
(B) Send him a notice
(C) Return the call
(D) Visit the office

10. How has the draft of the contract been sent?
(A) By post
(B) By e-mail
(C) By fax
(D) By express mail

Part 5

Choose the best answer to complete the sentence.

11. The Oregon Historic Preservation Committee ------- of twelve members, including professionals in the fields of history, architecture and archaeology.
(A) comprises (B) makes up (C) consists (D) composes

12. Dr. Chu's team has published a ------- article in an academic journal on editing human genomes.
(A) controvert (B) controversial (C) controversy (D) controversially

13. Delton Electronics achieved 12% growth in revenue for this fiscal year ------- downsizing an unprofitable department.
(A) due to (B) because (C) whether (D) but for

Part 6

Questions 14-17 refer to the following notice.

Everyone is invited!

Dingell Grocery Store is pleased to announce our Annual Fun Fair to be held in our parking lot on 8 May, from 10 A.M. to 5 P.M. This event is designed to entertain adults ------- children and is a great chance to spend time with your family.
14.

We'll ------- many street foods and special attractions. Enjoy everything from
15.
snacks children like, such as hotdogs and cotton candy, to international offerings such as kabobs and tacos. Try and win ------- with many games such as the soda
16.
pop toss and matching ducks game.

-------. So, come on foot and enjoy the sunshine. If it rains, the event will
17.
be held the next day.

---

14. (A) moreover
    (B) but
    (C) as well as
    (D) in addition

15. (A) providing
    (B) provided
    (C) provides
    (D) provide

16. (A) prizes
    (B) profits
    (C) benefits
    (D) gains

17. (A) Children under 12 are not allowed to join.
    (B) Don't bring your pets with you.
    (C) An attraction map will be posted at the entrance.
    (D) Please note that our usual parking lot is not available.

C CheckLink

Part 7

Questions 18-20 refer to the following text-message chain.

Jason Midlander [7:02 P.M.]
Marcia, this is Jason. We met yesterday in the lobby of the building. I just moved into the apartment next door.

Marcia Cardoso [7:24 P.M.]
Yes, I remember. From Kingston Valley, right?

Jason Midlander [7:27 P.M.]
No, Canyon Hills, that inconvenient suburb that never really developed.

Marcia Cardoso [7:29 P.M.]
Oh, right. What's up?

Jason Midlander [7:30 P.M.]
Is there a sporting goods store nearby? My daughter started playing tennis a few weeks ago and her coach suggested it's time for her to get her own racket.

Marcia Cardoso [7:32 P.M.]
What a coincidence. I work part-time at the local sporting goods store on weekends. It's just a five-minute walk from here.

Jason Midlander [7:33 P.M.]
No way! That's great. Could you help me out?

Marcia Cardoso [7:34 P.M.]
Sure.

Jason Midlander [7:35 P.M.]
What kind of racket do you recommend? My daughter really wants either a pink or orange one.

Marcia Cardoso [7:36 P.M.]
Yeah, those are very popular colors with girls. I'd suggest the Santos brand, but they're a bit more expensive.

Jason Midlander [7:37 P.M.]
What makes them more expensive?

Marcia Cardoso [7:39 P.M.]
Well, in particular, they are lighter and stronger. That's because of their titanium frame which is reinforced with carbon fiber. The racket should last a long time and provide a good base for her practice.

Jason Midlander [7:41 P.M.]
Wow, you really know your stuff. I'll bring my daughter along on Saturday. You're there this Saturday, aren't you?

> **Marcia Cardoso [7:42 P.M.]**
> Yeah, come on by and I'll help you find a racket. We have a sale on till Sunday.

> **Jason Midlander [7:42 P.M.]**
> Perfect. Thanks so much.

> **Marcia Cardoso [7:43 P.M.]**
> Sure, but I don't start till one in the afternoon.

> **Jason Midlander [7:43 P.M.]**
> OK. We'll make sure to come by after that.

> **Marcia Cardoso [7:43 P.M.]**
> I look forward to meeting the rest of your family.

18. Why does Mr. Midlander need a racket for his daughter?

(A) She is going to start playing tennis.

(B) The racket is her favorite color.

(C) Her coach thinks she should have one.

(D) There are some rackets on sale this week.

19. At 7:33 P.M., what does Mr. Midlander most likely mean when he writes, "That's great"?

(A) He expects Ms. Cardoso to give him some good advice.

(B) He is impressed by Ms. Cardoso's work environment.

(C) He plans to walk to a sporting goods store for his health.

(D) He is interested in working part-time in his neighborhood.

20. What is most likely true about Ms. Cardoso?

(A) She lived in an undeveloped suburb in Kingston Valley.

(B) She has a part-time job at a sports gear retailer.

(C) She is unfamiliar with the merchandise in her shop.

(D) She works the afternoon shift on weekdays.

Daily Life

Part **1**　ターゲット　1人の人物の写真問題に慣れよう

人物が1人だけ写っている写真問題はPart 1で基本の問題だ。まずはこのタイプの問題を確実に押さえよう。

Listen and fill in the blanks for each sentence. Then choose the statement that best describes what you see in the picture.

1.

CheckLink　DL 02　CD 1-06 ～ CD 1-10

(A) The man is (　　　　　　) (　　　) a table.

(B) The man is (　　　　　　) a (　　　　　　　　).

(C) The man is (　　　　　　) a piece of

(　　　　　　　).

(D) The man is (　　　　　) the (　　　　　　).

Choose the statement that best describes what you see in the picture.

2.

CheckLink　DL 03　CD 1-11

(A)　(B)　(C)　(D)

解法のポイント　人物の動作や着ているものに注目

音声が流れる前に、人物が立っているのか、前かがみなのか、あるいは寄りかかっているのか、また、半袖シャツを着ているのか、帽子をかぶっているのか、あるいは眼鏡をかけているのかなど、動作と身に着けているものに素早く注目しよう。日常生活で自分がしている動作や着用している衣服を英語でどう表現するのかを普段から意識して、オリジナルの表現集を作ってみるのもおススメだ。

Part 2 ターゲット 疑問詞を使った疑問文への応答文に慣れよう

whatやwhenなどの疑問詞を使った疑問文は、Part 2の25問中約11問出題されており、Part 2全体の約45%を占めている。疑問詞を正確に聞き取って、正しい答えを選ぼう。

Listen and fill in the blanks for each sentence. Then choose the best response to each question or statement.　CheckLink　DL 04 ~ 06　CD 1-12
CD 1-13 ~ CD 1-16

1. What time (　　　) (　　) (　　　　　) come to work?
   (A) (　　　　　) (　　　　), I think.
   (B) He is (　　　) (　　　　　　　).
   (C) Yes, he works (　　) (　　　　).

CD 1-17 ~ CD 1-20

2. (　　　　) (　　) you planning to (　　　　) (　　　) fixtures?
   (A) It's (　　　) (　　　　) (　　　) the plant.
   (B) (　　) (　) (　) (　　　　) lunchtime.
   (C) (　　　　) (　　　　) (　　) in the (　　　　　).

CD 1-21 ~ CD 1-24

3. Who _____
   _____ section?
   (A) Pablo is _____.
   (B) This detergent _____.
   (C) Mr. Chang _____
   _____.

Listen to the question or statement and the three responses. Then choose the best response.

4. (A)　(B)　(C)　CheckLink　DL 07　CD 1-25

解法のポイント 最初の疑問詞に集中する

Part 2では、質問文の冒頭に読み上げられる疑問詞に意識を集中して、絶対に聞き逃さないこと。ここを聞き逃してしまうと、せっかく他の応答文が全て聞こえても、正答を選べなくなってしまう。また、問われたことに対して的確な応答文を選べるように、Unit 1で様々な疑問詞を確認しておこう。

Choose the best answer to complete the sentence. ↻CheckLink

1. 名詞： Municipal officials urged thousands of ------- to evacuate immediately and also advised them to have a flashlight available during a blackout.

(A) resides (C) residence

(B) residents (D) residential

2. 動詞： The tenants of the apartment tried to ------- with their landlord about utilities being included in their rents.

(A) negotiate (C) negotiable

(B) negotiator (D) negotiation

3. 第1文型： The famous park is in the middle of an urban area, where various flowers ------- beautifully from season to season.

(A) plant (C) bear

(B) cultivate (D) bloom

4. 第3文型： Dwayne found a good apartment equipped with appliances, including a refrigerator, a microwave oven and light fixtures, but with no light bulbs, so he ------- a hardware store nearby.

(A) dropped (C) left

(B) visited (D) went

5. 第4文型： The real estate agent ------- us a property file and recommended some expensive condos overlooking the beautiful ocean.

(A) looked (C) showed

(B) saw (D) viewed

6. 形容詞： Ms. Curtis introduced a ------- plumber to me who she had asked before to repair the leaky water pipe under her kitchen sink.

(A) skill (C) skillful

(B) skillfulness (D) skillfully

7. 第2文型：This fabric is so ------- that you should use a special laundry detergent and softener to maintain its original texture.

(A) delicacy

(B) delicate

(C) delicately

(D) delicatessen

8. 第5文型：The gardener ------- their patio beautiful by periodically mowing the lawn and trimming the trees.

(A) keeps

(B) make

(C) maintaining

(D) who leaves

9. 副詞：Every Sunday morning Jessica washes their clothes and hangs them out, and in the afternoon her husband takes in the laundry and folds it -------.

(A) neat

(B) neaten

(C) neatness

(D) neatly

10. 語彙：Sonterra Foods Ltd. is one of the nation's largest companies that supplies ------- products such as cheese, butter and yogurt.

(A) dairy

(B) diary

(C) daily

(D) delay

解法のポイント 機械的な対処法が重要

Part 5 に割ける時間は全30問で10分、1問あたり20秒しかなく、選択肢を一つ一つ当てはめながら和訳して…とガッツリ正面から取り組むやり方ではまず間に合わない。また、品詞・語形を問う問題は30問中約33%（10問前後）と実にPart 5の3分の1を占めているので、軽視できない。空所に求められている品詞を即座に見抜いて選択肢の品詞を即座に見分けるという、機械的な対処法の習得が絶対的に必要だ。

Part 7には全部で23個の資料が出てくるが、メール形式は最も数が多く、平均7個出題されている。注目すべき箇所を押さえて、要領よく処理しよう。

Questions 1-4 refer to the following e-mail.

CheckLink

Date:	March 1
To:	Timothy Colley
From:	Gwen Diaz
Subject:	Request for Repairs

Dear Mr. Colley,

I rent a house at 12 Harborne Lane, Wembley, and have been your tenant for the last three years. I am writing to you to request some repairs to the property.

The staircase rail to the upper floor has grown very loose and needs to be fixed. This is an accident waiting to happen, and I especially worry for the safety of my kids. The toilet has started to clog constantly, and I have tried very hard to fix it every time it happens. I am afraid the pipe needs a full inspection by a professional plumber. Also, the gas stove that you kindly installed in the kitchen when we moved in suddenly stopped working last week. According to our lease agreement, I believe the owner is responsible for repairs and maintenance of the building, plumbing system, and equipped appliances. I would appreciate it if you could contact me as soon as possible to discuss arrangements for repairs.

I can be reached at 902-354-1986. Please leave a message if I cannot answer, and I will get back to you. I would like to have them fixed as soon as possible because I am expecting guests in three weeks for a one-week stay. I will need notice of the date and time for repairs so that I can arrange to be home. I would like the people in charge of repairs to refrain from entering the house without me being there.

Thank you for attending to this, and I am looking forward to hearing from you soon.

Sincerely,
Gwen Diaz

1. Who is Mr. Colley?

(A) A house owner

(B) A real estate agent

(C) A repair worker

(D) A lawyer

2. Why is Ms. Diaz worried about the staircase rail?

(A) Her children cannot reach the upper floor.

(B) It is too expensive to fix.

(C) Her children might get injured.

(D) She is trying to fix it by herself.

3. What is indicated about the stove?

(A) It has been out of order for three years.

(B) It is the only cooking appliance in the kitchen.

(C) The house was equipped with it three years ago.

(D) Ms. Diaz brought it from another place.

4. According to Ms. Diaz, what will happen later this month?

(A) Repairs will be completed.

(B) Visitors will stay with her.

(C) She will move out for repairs.

(D) She will visit Mr. Colley.

解法のポイント いきなり本文から読まない

Single passageの問題は10題出題される。本問のような4つの設問付きの問題の1題あたりの解答時間は5分強しかなく、気持ちが焦ってしまうが、メールの問題ではメールの受信者・送信者・日付・件名に目を通してから本文に入った方が、2人の関係性がつかみやすい。

UNIT 2 Shopping

Part 1　ターゲット　何が写っているのかをよく観察しよう

Part 1の問題では、写真に写っている人物や物を正しく描写する選択肢を選ばなければならない。音声が流れる前に、写真をじっくり見ておこう。

Listen and fill in the blanks for each sentence. Then choose the statement that best describes what you see in the picture.

1. CheckLink　DL 08　CD 1-26 ~ CD 1-30

(A) A man is (　　　　　) a
(　　　　　　　　) from a
(　　　　　　).

(B) A man is (　　　　　　　)
(　　　) (　　　　).

(C) A man is (　　　　　) a
(　　　　　　　　)
(　　　　　　).

(D) A man is (　　　　　) a
(　　　　　　　) (　　　　　　).

Choose the statement that best describes what you see in the picture.

2. CheckLink　DL 09　CD 1-31

(A)　(B)　(C)　(D)

解法のポイント　写真に写っていないものはすぐに排除する

写真に写っていない人物や物、動作などが聞こえた瞬間に、その選択肢は排除して構わない。そうやって確実に不正解の選択肢を除いて、残る候補から答えを選ぶことによって、当然のことだが、正答率はアップする。

Part 3 ターゲット 設問と選択肢を先読みしよう

会話が流れてくる前に、あらかじめ設問と選択肢に目を通すように心がけよう。速読・即解するのが苦手なら、設問に目を通すだけでもよい。

Listen to the conversation and fill in the blanks. Then choose the best answer to each question. ↻CheckLink 🎧 DL 10 ◉CD 1-32 ~ ◉CD 1-36

W: Hello, Springfield Clothing (**1.**   ). You've reached

   (**2.**   ) (**3.**   ). How may I help you?

M: I recently bought a (**4.**   ) pullover on sale online, but it's (**5.**   )

   (**6.**   ) for me. Do you have the same one in large? If you don't, I'd like to

   (**7.**   ) my (**8.**   ).

W: (**9.**   ), the large-sized pullover is (**10.**   ) (**11.**)

   (**12.**   ) and we are not sure when we'll get a shipment. We are sorry, but

   (**13.**   ) (**14.**   ) return such as having ordered the (**15.**   )

   (**16.**   ) are regarded as a return (**17.**   ) (**18.**) a customer's

   (**19.**   ) preference.

M: Oh, no, that's a problem. That means I'm (**20.**   ) for

   (**21.**   ) fees, right? Well, I don't have a (**22.**   ).

🎧 DL 11 ◉CD 1-37

1. Who most likely is the woman?

   (A) A shop clerk

   (B) A customer service representative

   (C) A sales manager

   (D) A public relations staff

2. What problem does the man mention?

   (A) He ordered a small-sized pullover.

   (B) He got the product in a wrong color.

   (C) He has not received his purchase yet.

   (D) He could not buy the company's stock.

3. What does the man imply he will do?

   (A) Return the product

   (B) Purchase the item again

   (C) Place a backorder

   (D) Charge the woman a fee

Listen to the conversation and choose the best answer to each question.

CheckLink   DL 12, 13   CD 1-38 ~ CD 1-43   CD 1-44

4. What are the speakers mainly discussing?

   (A) Whether to renew subscriptions

   (B) Whether to publish a new journal

   (C) Whether to cut the budget for printing

   (D) Whether to subscribe to a newspaper

5. Why does Mark agree with the woman?

   (A) They can get a discount on online newspapers.

   (B) They can read digital issues for free.

   (C) They can cut down on their spending.

   (D) They can contribute an article.

6. What is the woman probably going to do next?

   (A) Submit an academic paper

   (B) Send information to subscribers

   (C) Apply for a grant

   (D) Use the Internet

解法のポイント　先読みのメリット

設問を前もって読んでいれば、設問が読み上げられる時間を待たずに、会話を聞きながら答えを選ぶことができるし、設問や選択肢に含まれる語句から、これから流れてくる内容や流れをある程度予測することもできるので、高得点を狙うには先読みはマスト。directions や設問が読み上げられる時間を上手に利用して、あらかじめ設問と選択肢に目を通す先読みパターンを身に付けよう。

Part 6　ターゲット　時短を心がけよう

Part 6に割ける時間は全体で8分、1題あたり2分しかない。Part 5で出題されるような、内容を読み込まなくても文法的に処理できる問題は、文構造を的確にとらえて、求められている正解を即座に見抜けるようになろう。

Questions **1-4** refer to the following Webpage.

Send Feedback, Get Voucher!

Donna & Taylor is always looking for ways to improve our service as well as to help customers have satisfying experiences shopping with ------- . To help
1.
others make smart choices and confident decisions on our website, share your

thoughts or ------- on the product you have purchased by writing a review.
2.
Answering the online questionnaire will only take a few minutes. Just log

into "MY ACCOUNT" and rate a product. All information we collect is kept

------- . As a small token of our appreciation, you will be entered in a monthly
3.
draw to win a $500 gift card. Each review you write has a chance for entry.

------- .
4.

---

1. (A) us　　　　　　　(C) you

　　(B) them　　　　　　(D) it

2. (A) sensibility　　　　(C) manners

　　(B) speech　　　　　(D) opinions

3. (A) secure　　　　　　(C) securing

　　(B) security　　　　　(D) securely

4. (A) The stores where you can get it are limited.

　　(B) We are not ready to deliver gifts yet.

　　(C) Don't let this rare opportunity slip away.

　　(D) Our newly released products are not available now.

解法のポイント 時間配分を常に意識すること

TOEIC® L&R の対策を始めたばかりの頃は、1題を2分で解くのはなかなか難しい。まずは出題形式に慣れることを目標にし、それから時間配分を意識して解くようにしよう。時間配分や要領がつかめるまでは、Part 6の文挿入問題はひとまずマークだけしておき、次の問題に進むのもアリだ。

メール、ウェブページ、オンラインチャットやテキストメッセージ以外は、パッと見ただけでは文書の形式が分かりづらい。これら以外の文書では、まず本文の上 (枠外) の導入部 Questions xx-xx refer to the following ○○. に注目しよう。○○には、advertisement、article、notice、press release など、これから読む文書がどのような形式なのかが表わされている。この導入部を見て心の準備をしておくと、内容に入りやすくなる。

Questions 1-4 refer to the following advertisement.　　　　　　　 ↻ CheckLink

Millini&co.

Special Launch Event
Bohemian Line of Bags
Noon-6 P.M., Sunday, March 21

Are you ready to feel the luxury of our European handbags? The Bohemian Line is making its national debut this week. Coming to you from the luxury boutiques of Paris and Milan.

Visit our downtown store to see what all the fashion magazines are talking about. Feel the quality that has become associated with the Millini&co. brand. The reviews have been fabulous. The chief designer, Ms. Vanutti will present about the Bohemian Line at 4 P.M.

Take advantage of this event to purchase your piece of portable heaven. Special offers are available for all products on this day. If your selection is out of stock, we will guarantee that your item is delivered to you overnight by express mail.

Everyone is invited to this very special event. What are you waiting for? Make plans to visit us on March 21. Bring a friend and enjoy our complimentary refreshments.

Millini&co.
2583 Main Street
Tel: 793-5729
Mon.-Fri. 9 A.M.-9 P.M. (10 P.M. on Saturdays)
Closed on Sundays

1. For whom is this advertisement intended?

    (A) Prospective customers

    (B) The staff of Millini&co.

    (C) Suppliers

    (D) Event organizers

2. What is Ms. Vanutti going to do on March 21?

    (A) Speak about the fashion world

    (B) Give a special offer

    (C) Talk about the advertised item

    (D) Present customers with bags she designed

3. What is NOT suggested about the event?

    (A) Visitors will be able to check out the new product.

    (B) Some fashion magazines will cover the event.

    (C) The event will take place on a store holiday.

    (D) The Bohemian Line will be sold at a reduced price.

4. What will be offered to the participants in the event for free?

    (A) Handbags

    (B) Product samples

    (C) Shipping and handling

    (D) Light snacks and drinks

解法のポイント **Part 7 の時間配分に慣れるまでは…**

Single passage は 10 題を 25 分以内で解かなければならないが、頭では分かっていてもなかなかそのペースを守るのは大変だ。Part 7 の時間配分に慣れるまでは、解答に時間がかかる「NOT 問題」と「文挿入問題」は飛ばしてもよい。もちろん、その場合もマークだけはしておくことを忘れないように。

Parties & Events

Part 1　ターゲット　複数人物の写真問題に慣れよう

Part 1の写真描写問題6問中、複数の人物が写っている問題は2～3問出題されている。複数人物の問題に慣れよう。

Listen and fill in the blanks for each sentence. Then choose the statement that best describes what you see in the picture.

1.

CheckLink　DL 14　CD 1-45 ～ CD 1-49

(A) (　　　　　) are (　　　　　　　) at the
(　　　　　　　).

(B) (　　　　　) are (　　　　　　) the
merchandise over the (　　　　　　).

(C) (　　　　) of the (　　　　) is (　　　　　　)
on a cap.

(D) (　　　　) of the (　　　　) is (　　　　　　)
at a TV screen.

Choose the statement that best describes what you see in the picture.

2.

CheckLink　DL 15　CD 1-50

(A)　(B)　(C)　(D)

解法のポイント　主語を聞き取って、共通の動作に注目

複数の人物が写っている問題では、写真全体を広く見ながら、音声の主語の部分にすばやく反応して焦点を合わせる。もし読まれた主語がTheyやThe menなどの両者もしくは全員を指す語（句）の場合は、目立つ動作に釣られないで、全員に共通の動作を探すこと。

Part 4 ターゲット 「誰が、誰に、どこで話しているか」をつかもう

話の内容だけでなく、どういった状況での発話なのかを判断することが設問に解答する上では大切。どこで話されているのか、話し手と聞き手は誰なのか、また、話し手と聞き手の関係はどのようなものか。"Attention, passengers."、"Good afternoon, shoppers."、"Welcome, new managers." などの呼びかけから、自ずと聞き手や状況が特定される場合もあるが、そうでない場合は、内容から聞き手や状況を自分で推測する力が必要。

Listen to the short talk and fill in the blanks. Then choose the best answer to each question. CheckLink DL 16 CD 1-51 ~ CD 1-54

Welcome, everyone, to our annual (1.) gala dinner here at Pan Pacific Hotel. The funds we collect this evening will benefit the (2.) project of the historic Huntington (3.). As you know, our fund-raising goal is (4.) (5.) dollars. (6.) (7.) (8.), I'd like to (9.) this wonderful hotel for generously donating the meal you're about to enjoy. Also, (10.) (11.) (12.) (13.) (14.) our business (15.) listed on the back of your program. They (16.) our mission of conserving our cultural heritage for future (17.). (18.) (19.), we'll hear from today's (20.) (21.), Professor Anna De Rossi. Professor De Rossi will be speaking about the historical and architectural significance of Huntington Theater and the (22.) of its restoration project.

DL 17 CD 1-55

1. What is mentioned about Huntington Theater?
(A) It is the venue for this event.
(B) It is being restored.
(C) It will be replaced by a new theater.
(D) It will be relocated.

2. What does the speaker say was offered by Pan Pacific Hotel?
(A) Food
(B) 15 million dollars
(C) Theater tickets
(D) Programs

3. What will the listeners most likely do next?
(A) Talk to their sponsors
(B) Eat dinner
(C) Celebrate the anniversary
(D) Visit Huntington Theater

Listen to the short talk and choose the best answer to each question.

CheckLink 　DL 18, 19 　CD 1-56 ~ 　CD 1-59 　CD 1-60

4. What is the message mainly about?

(A) Availability of food ingredients (C) Suggestions for recipes

(B) Healthy diets (D) Inquiries and requests about food

5. Which food item in the original order will remain the same after the alterations?

(A) Non-vegetarian meals (C) Cold beverages

(B) Vegetarian meals (D) Coffee

6. Who is Phil Blaney?

(A) One of the speaker's colleagues (C) A delivery truck driver

(B) A catering company manager (D) A food magazine publisher

解法のポイント　音声の順番で設問に取り組む

Part 4は一人が長く話すタイプの音声問題なので、全てを聞き取るのは難しく、*TOEIC*® L&Rに慣れていない人は途中で聞き取りを諦めてしまいがちだ。しかし基本的に、設問は読まれる音声の順に出題されるので、音声を聞く前に設問を読んでおくようにすれば、聞き取れた部分に関する設問だけでも解答することができ、正答率を上げることができる。

Part 5 　ターゲット　形容詞と副詞の働きをマスターしよう

Choose the best answer to complete the sentence. 　CheckLink

1. 形容詞の限定用法：Derek Pearl, one of the most famous children's book authors, made a ------- donation to the charity through World Book Fund for Children.

(A) general (B) generous (C) generally (D) generosity

2. 形容詞の限定用法：With sponsorship from a local catering company, party attendees could enjoy a wide range of ------- refreshments provided at the venue.

(A) complete (B) complement (C) compliment (D) complimentary

3. 形容詞の叙述用法：The authentic Italian cuisine served at the restaurant where our annual party took place the other day tasted so -------.

(A) good (B) flavor (C) deliciously (D) well

4. 動詞を修飾する副詞：Exposed to the weather and liable to suffer deterioration, the open-air stadium is ------- restored.

(A) regular   (B) regularity   (C) regularly   (D) regulation

5. 形容詞を修飾する副詞：The pre-grand opening event of the shopping complex will feature a fashion show by young designers who are ------- creative and the most notable now.

(A) real   (B) realize   (C) reality   (D) really

6. 接続副詞：Admission to the special exhibition at the National Museum of Art was rather expensive at twenty-five dollars; ------- there was an endless line of visitors every day.

(A) nevertheless   (B) moreover   (C) consequently   (D) otherwise

7. 形容詞と副詞：I managed to get just one ticket for my favorite singer's upcoming tour and I can ------- wait to go.

(A) hard   (B) hardly   (C) harden   (D) hardness

8. 形容詞と副詞：In order to renovate its facility in commemoration of the 70th anniversary, Jackson Theater has hosted some fund-raising events and ------- achieved the target figure.

(A) late   (B) lateness   (C) latest   (D) lately

9. 語彙：The performances of all the actors and actresses were so ------- that they received a roaring standing ovation from the entire audience.

(A) aggressive   (B) depressive   (C) impressive   (D) progressive

10. 語彙：Abigale ------- the Hawaiian restaurant for Ms. O'Connell's farewell party because she likes its casual atmosphere.

(A) deserved   (B) observed   (C) reserved   (D) preserved

┃**解法のポイント**┃ 形容詞・副詞が問われる問題では位置が重要

品詞問題で頻出する形は、〈冠詞＋形容詞＋名詞〉や〈助動詞＋副詞＋動詞の原形〉〈be動詞＋副詞＋動詞の過去分詞〉のように、間に「形容詞」や「副詞」が入っているタイプだ。さらに発展形として、〈the most＋形容詞＋名詞〉や〈冠詞＋副詞＋形容詞＋名詞〉などがある。

本問のような5つの設問付きの double passage 問題は2題出題されるが、割ける時間は2題で12分、1題あたり6分しかない。要領よく取り組もう。

Questions 1-5 refer to the following Webpage and e-mail. 　　　　　**C** CheckLink

The Super Generous Foundation of Tokyo ×　+

◀ ▶ C　🔒 http://www.supergenerousft.org/　　　　　👤 ⋮

The Super Generous Foundation of Tokyo (SGFT)

| Home | **Events** | Offerings | Contact Us |

The Third National Charity Week (NCW-3) Call for Charity Event Organizers

Dates:
- ➤ charity week from 1st to 5th October

Entry Qualifications:
- ➤ an individual or group

Types of Events:
- ➤ musical entertainment
- ➤ food-service activity
- ➤ public sale of goods
- ➤ sporting participation

Support from our event assistance consultant available*:
- ➤ budget control
- ➤ facility operation
- ➤ effective publicity

Contribution Destination:
- ➤ children's hospitals with financial problems in our city

For further information and registration** e-mail to:
Mark Aggawal at maggawal@supergenerousft.com

Notes:

* This service is only for first-time organizers.

** For registration, you need to include your background information, what types of event(s) you want to hold, how many people you expect to attend the event(s), and where you want to hold the event(s).

To:	Mark Aggawal <maggawal@supergenerousft.com>
From:	Thomas Takeda <thtakeda@meishi.ac.jp>
Subject:	Charity event organizer
Date:	March 13

Dear Mr. Aggawal,

I am writing to apply as an organizer for the Third National Charity Week. I am currently studying community medicine policy at Meishi University. Also, I am the president of the charity club of our university. Our club has been looking for a practical approach to contributing to our city's regional medicine policy. This is our first time to apply for the project, so there must still be many things we have to learn about.

Our plan includes an outdoor mini-concert with complimentary beverages, a bazaar, and an auction of artwork created by local children. For the bazaar and auction, the northern section of the park near the university can be a candidate venue. For the mini-concert, a small hall at our university has been renovated recently. Participants would not be inconvenienced because the venues are close to each other.

I really hope we are chosen and can join the project. I am looking forward to hearing from you.

Best regards,

Thomas Takeda

1. What is the purpose of the webpage?

    (A) To find charity event organizers

    (B) To improve a children's playground

    (C) To hold a charity concert

    (D) To hire a new consultant

2. To whom will the money collected at the charity events go?

    (A) Children's hospitals in the city

    (B) Charity programs for public schools

    (C) NPOs in the city

    (D) Clubs at Meishi University

3. If Mr. Takeda's group is chosen, what kind of benefits can it receive?

    (A) It can receive financial help.

    (B) It can work as a consultant of SGFT.

    (C) It can get assistance for promoting the events.

    (D) It can acquire a scholarship from the university.

4. In the e-mail, the word "complimentary" in paragraph 2, line 1, is closest in meaning to

    (A) feasible

    (B) healthy

    (C) free

    (D) implicit

5. What required information did Mr. Takeda fail to include in his e-mail?

    (A) His background information

    (B) The types of events

    (C) The candidate sites for the events

    (D) The number of potential participants

解法のポイント 解答時間を意識すること

Single passage 同様、「①本文の上の枠外にある導入部→②本文のタイトルや1行目→③設問→④本文」の順番に目を通して、要領よく解き進めよう。また、両方の文書を読まないと解けない問題もあるが、設問1〜2は1つ目の文書を参照する問題、設問3〜5は2つ目の文書を参照する問題と両方の文書を参照する問題となっていることが多いというのも覚えておくと役に立つ。

今の大学生にとって必要な*TOEIC*® L&R その勉強をすることの意味とは①

　TOEIC® L&Rのスコアは、大学の単位の認定に活用されたり、進級や卒業の要件として設定されたりしています。そして、採用試験では応募者の英語能力を測るものとして、また企業では社員の昇進・昇格や海外出張・駐在の要件として広く採用されています。その理由として、①他の英語の資格試験と比べて安価である、②試験回数が多く受験しやすい、③幅のある級ではなくスコアで英語力を測ることができる、などが挙げられ、学生だけでなく、多くの社会人も*TOEIC*® L&Rのスコアアップを目指して日々勉強をしています。

中高で学んだ内容＋αが求められるテスト

　TOEIC® L&Rで扱われている内容は日常の場面からビジネスまで多岐にわたります。リスニングでは職場での会話や交通機関の案内、リーディングではレストランのメニューや様々な広告、時刻表や社内文書などがあり、中高での授業では接する機会が少なかった分野に関する内容が多くなります。スコアアップを目指すには、まず、これまでに学んだ英単語に加えて、そういった分野の語彙を増やさなければなりません。さらに、アメリカ英語だけでなく、イギリス英語、カナダ英語、オーストラリア英語も使用されているので、それぞれの英語の特徴をつかみ、聞き取る力をアップさせることも重要です。

　また、特にリーディングセクションでは、正確な英文法の知識も求められます。*TOEIC*® L&Rにおける文法の知識を問う問題は、高校や大学の入学試験のものとは異なります。それらに対応できる力を身に付けるためにも、大学生としてのより一歩進んだ幅広い文法の勉強が必要になってきます。

Traffic & Travel

Part 1の写真描写問題6問中、人物が写っていない風景写真の問題は1〜2問出題されている。風景の写真問題に慣れよう。

Listen and fill in the blanks for each sentence. Then choose the statement that best describes what you see in the picture.

1.

CheckLink 　 DL 20 　 CD 1-61 〜 CD 1-65

(A) Some (   ) are
    (   ) at an
    (   ).

(B) Some (   ) are being
    (   ) in the
    (   ).

(C) Some automobiles are (   )
    (   ) the (   ).

(D) Some construction (   )
    are (   ) low (   ).

Choose the statement that best describes what you see in the picture.

2.

CheckLink 　 DL 21 　 CD 1-66

(A)　(B)　(C)　(D)

人物が写っていない風景の写真問題では、人物を描写する選択肢を候補から外せるため、選択肢を絞り込みやすいという利点がある一方で、写真の一部に意識を集中できないという難点もある。複数の人物が写っている問題と同様に、写真全体を広く見ながら、音声が流れたら言及された物にすばやく反応して焦点を当て、写真と音声を比べよう。

Part 2 〔ターゲット〕 英語の音声変化に慣れよう

Part 2で流れる英文は短文なので、ついて行くのが大変ということはないが、単語と単語がつながって発音されたり（連結）、単語と単語がつながって別の音に変化したり（同化）、本来ある音が発音されなくなったり（脱落）するので、音の変化にうまく対応できないと、知っているはずの単語も聞き取れなくなってしまう。

Listen and fill in the blanks for each sentence. Then choose the best response to each question or statement. ↻CheckLink 🎧 DL 22 ~ 24 ◉CD 1-67 ◉CD 1-68 ~ ◉CD 1-71

1. Are there (　　) (　　) (　　) (　　)?
   (A) (　　) (　　) (　　); one (　　) please.
   (B) Yes, I'll (　　) you (　　) (　　) (　　).
   (C) You (　　) (　　) (　　) (　　) he will be available.

◉CD 1-72 ~ ◉CD 1-75

2. (　　) (　　) (　　) is a souvenir shop, isn't (　)?
   (A) No, the (　　) (　　) (　　).
   (B) Yes, (　　) (　　) (　　).
   (C) The (　　) (　　) (　　).

◉CD 1-76 ~ ◉CD 1-79

3. _____ payment to the travel agency for the difference?
   (A) I'm sure your _____.
   (B) No, you have to _____.
   (C) I _____, but _____.

Listen to the question or statement and the three responses. Then choose the best response.

4. (A) (B) (C) ↻CheckLink 🎧 DL 25 ◉CD 1-80

〔解法のポイント〕 リピーティングやディクテーションなどで対策を

変化する音声は「連結」や「同化」、「脱落」の他に、フラッピング（母音に挟まれたtの音がrやdに変化）もあるが、ある程度パターン化されている。解答後に正解の英文を使ってリピーティングやシャドーイング、ディクテーションを行い、自分が苦手とする音声変化のパターンを克服しよう。

Choose the best answer to complete the sentence.　ⒸCheckLink

1. 前置詞：Hermione checked her baggage at the check-in counter, and was waiting
------- the baggage claim at her destination, but it didn't appear.

(A) for

(B) at

(C) under

(D) through

2. 前置詞：Unfortunately, all accommodations in the downtown area were fully
booked ------- the Christmas season, so we couldn't find any twin rooms.

(A) between

(B) among

(C) while

(D) during

3. 前置詞：A vehicle hit a pedestrian walking on the crosswalk on Tremont Avenue
------- the night of November 18.

(A) at

(B) in

(C) on

(D) to

4. 群前置詞：------- to the timetable, a bus comes every five minutes around this time.

(A) According

(B) Thanks

(C) In addition

(D) With a view

5. 群前置詞：------- their expectations, the souvenir is gathering attention on the
Internet and is selling like hotcakes.

(A) But for

(B) Contrary to

(C) Except for

(D) Owing to

6. 群前置詞：After it was announced that all domestic flights had been canceled
------- the heavy snow, about six hundred passengers were stranded overnight at
the airport.

(A) as to

(B) instead of

(C) due to

(D) regardless of

7. **群前置詞**：Commuting by public transportation is more eco-friendly ------- energy efficiency and CO₂ emissions, and healthier because you can burn more than twice as many calories.

(A) in charge of　　　　(C) in spite of

(B) in front of　　　　(D) in terms of

8. **語彙**：Brandon reserved a package tour on the travel agency's website and called them to ------- his reservation just in case.

(A) conceal　　　　(C) conquer

(B) confirm　　　　(D) convert

9. **語彙**：All the drivers heading for Oakland City Hall have to ------- a detour because the highway is under construction.

(A) catch　　　　(C) have

(B) get　　　　(D) make

10. **語彙**：Mr. and Ms. Onoda flew to Paris from Tokyo ------- Singapore instead of using a direct flight so as to earn miles.

(A) by way of　　　　(C) in the way of

(B) by the way　　　　(D) on the way to

解法のポイント 意味が似ている前置詞を区別しよう

during や for、among は使い方や意味が異なるが、全て「～の間」と和訳することができてしまう。また、by や until [till] はどちらも「～まで」と和訳することができてしまう。反対に、「～について」の意味をもつ前置詞には about だけでなく、of や on、with などがある。細かい違いや同じ意味の表現は、まとめて覚えるのが得策だ。

テキストメッセージやオンラインチャット形式の問題は、Part 7の23個の資料中、毎回2つ出題されている。特徴をつかんで、適切に処理しよう。

Questions 1-4 refer to the following text-message chain.

ⵊ CheckLink

● ● ● 👤 Emily 👤 Eric 👤 Kylie ‹ ›

Emily Maughan [9:55 A.M.]
Hi, Eric, are you in the office? Due to airport congestion, the airplane cannot take off. As soon as it arrives at the airport, I'll catch a taxi. My presentation at the monthly meeting is scheduled for 13:00. I'll be in time for it, but I'll have no time to prepare. Will you set up the devices in the meeting room? The meeting room will be available after 11:30.

Eric Sparkes [9:56 A.M.]
Sorry, I'm leaving the office soon. I have an appointment with a client. Kylie, do you have time?

Kylie Corden [10:01 A.M.]
No problem. I'll set up the projector and the PC and place the documents on the desks.

Emily Maughan [10:02 A.M.]
Thanks. And then, would you put cups, plates, cutlery and paper napkins on the table near the door? The caterer will deliver snacks and beverages in two hours. Would you receive them and arrange them on the table?

Kylie Corden [10:03 A.M.]
I'll do it.

Kylie Corden [10:10 A.M.]
Emily, I cannot find the handouts. Have you already prepared them?

Eric Sparkes [10:11 A.M.]
Did you look in the file cabinet next to the copier? They should be there. If not, print them out and staple them.

> **Kylie Corden [10:13 A.M.]**
> They weren't there. I'll begin that work in a while.

> **Emily Maughan [10:15 A.M.]**
> I forgot—I haven't printed them out yet. You can do it from our shared files. Tentatively, everything is going well. Thanks everyone. The plane's taking off. See you soon.

1. What does Ms. Maughan ask for?

  (A) The departure time of her plane   (C) Some help with her presentation

  (B) The cancellation of the meeting   (D) A reservation for a taxi

2. At 9:56 A.M., what does Mr. Sparkes most likely mean when he writes, "Sorry"?

  (A) He made a mistake about his departure time.

  (B) He cannot meet Ms. Maughan's request.

  (C) He will be late for the meeting.

  (D) He cannot make a presentation.

3. What will Ms. Corden do around noon?

  (A) Meet a client   (C) Hand in a report

  (B) Sign a document   (D) Receive catering

4. What will Ms. Corden most likely do next?

  (A) Go shopping for certain folders

  (B) Contact the caterer

  (C) Prepare papers

  (D) Search the presentation handouts

解法のポイント　オンラインチャットやテキストメッセージ形式の問題の特色をつかむ

オンラインチャットやテキストメッセージは、文字化された会話文と考えればよい。実際、Part 3で出題される「午前／午後○○時○○分に△△が□□と書く際、何を意図していると考えられますか」という形式の設問が、毎回出題されている。また、2人で行われるやりとりと3人以上で行われるやりとりがあるが、3人以上のやりとりでは、発言者が誰であるかを追うよりも、話題を追った方が解答につながる場合が多い。話題の移り変わりに注意して読み進めよう。

Office Work

Part 1　ターゲット　聞こえた単語に惑わされないようにしよう

慣れないうちは聞き取れた単語だけを頼りに答えを選んでしまいがちだが、関連がありそうな単語やフレーズを使って、受験者を惑わせようとする「引っ掛け」問題もあるので気をつけよう。

Listen and fill in the blanks for each sentence. Then choose the statement that best describes what you see in the picture.

1.

⟳CheckLink　⬇DL 26　◎CD 2-01 ～ ◎CD 2-05

(A) The woman is (　　　　) a
　　(　　　　).
(B) The woman is (　　　　)
　　(　　　) a phone call.
(C) The woman is (　　　　)
　　(　　　　) memorandums.
(D) The woman is (　　　) next to
　　her (　　　　).

Choose the statement that best describes what you see in the picture.

2.　⟳CheckLink　⬇DL 27　◎CD 2-06

(A)　(B)　(C)　(D)

解法のポイント　あせらず最後まで聞く

主語と動作までは写真と合っている選択肢も、続く動作の対象（目的語）や場所が異なっていれば、当然不正解である。音声の途中で答えを選ばず、全ての選択肢を最後までちゃんと聞いてから答えを選ぼう。また、写真を見て答える Part 1では、英文を聞いて和訳するのではなく、その英文が表現する内容を映像でイメージする癖をつけるとよい。

Part 3 ターゲット 図表付き会話問題に慣れよう

図表付き会話問題は Part 3 の後半に 3 題出題されるが、図表はシンプルな作りのスケジュールやグラフ、チケットやクーポンなどなので、気負わずに取り組もう。

Listen to the conversation and fill in the blanks. Then choose the best answer to each question. CheckLink DL 28 CD 2-07 ~ CD 2-11

M: Are you the moderator of the (1.   )? I've just been informed that Ms. Harper is unable to (2.   ) a (3.   ) today as she has an (4.   ) (5.   ).

W: Oh, no! She is the (6.   ) (7.   )! The (8.   ) is (9.   ) to (10.   ) at nine thirty, so I'll (11.   ) notify the (12.   ) about her cancellation and (13.   ) the (14.   ) of the workshop.

M: (15.   ), would you start the workshop as planned? I talked with Mr. Buchanan, the second speaker, and he is willing to (16.   ) (17.   ) (18.   ) her and will be presenting first.

W: (19.   ) (20.   ). Anyhow Ms. Harper has (21.   ), so the workshop session will finish ahead of schedule. We can (22.   ) more time for questions and answers.

DL 29 CD 2-12

1. What is the trouble?
   (A) Ms. Harper was asked unexpectedly to make a presentation.
   (B) Mr. Buchanan cannot participate in the workshop.
   (C) Mr. Buchanan has to delay the schedule.
   (D) Ms. Harper cannot come to the workshop.

2. Why does the man say, "would you start the workshop as planned"?
   (A) To suggest an alternative plan
   (B) To inform the woman of Mr. Buchanan's rejection
   (C) To offer to stand in for Ms. Harper
   (D) To confirm the original time schedule

3. Why does the woman think they can have a longer Q&A time?
   (A) All the speakers will make their presentations shorter.
   (B) More participants will come to the workshop session.
   (C) The workshop session will finish earlier than originally scheduled.
   (D) Mr. Buchanan will show up late for the workshop session.

Listen to the conversation while looking at the chart and choose the best answer to each question. ⟳CheckLink ⬇ DL 30, 31 ⊙ CD 2-13 ~ ⊙ CD 2-19 ⊙ CD 2-20

Main Conference Room		
Time	Department	Purpose
10:00 A.M. - 11:30 A.M.	R&D	Weekly Team Meeting
11:30 A.M. - 12:30 P.M.		Main Conference Room is available at this time
12:30 P.M. - 2:30 P.M.	Sales	Lunch Meeting
2:30 P.M. - 5:30 P.M.		Main Conference Room is available at this time

4. What is the woman doing now?

(A) Making copies of letters

(B) Reserving a meeting room

(C) Repairing the photocopier

(D) Preparing documents for the meeting

5. Look at the graphic. When is the man in the main conference room?

(A) 10:00 A.M. - 11:30 A.M.   (C) 12:30 P.M. - 2:30 P.M.

(B) 11:30 A.M. - 12:30 P.M.   (D) 2:30 P.M. - 5:30 P.M.

6. What does the woman want Patrick to do?

(A) Attend the morning meeting

(B) Ask for Ashley's contact information

(C) Travel abroad on business

(D) Go through the report

解法のポイント 設問、選択肢、図表の先読みが必要

Part 3では1つの会話につき3つの設問が出されるが、図表問題ではその3つのうち1つは、"Look at the graphic."で始まる設問になっている。設問と選択肢をある程度先読みすることが大切なのはUnit 2でも述べたが、図表問題では先読みの時に図表も一緒にチェックしてほしい。このタイプの問題では、具体的な場所、時間や数字などを問われるので、関連する情報を聞き逃さないこと。

Part 5 ターゲット 接続詞をマスターしよう

Choose the best answer to complete the sentence. ⟲CheckLink

1. 接続詞： ------- you often work overtime or through lunch to meet deadlines, you should review your procedures.

(A) As (C) But

(B) That (D) Until

2. 接続詞： ------- you make your subordinates get their priorities straight, they won't be able to deal with their work efficiently.

(A) Once (C) If

(B) Since (D) Unless

3. 相関接続詞：Ms. Rodrigo is not our receptionist ------- our Florida sales representative.

(A) and (C) so

(B) but (D) though

4. 相関接続詞：My supervisor told neither Frederic ------- me to give a lecture at the annual conference on how to improve customer service.

(A) and (C) or

(B) but (D) nor

5. 接続詞： ------- I can remember, approximately 40 people attended the in-house seminar on presentation skills.

(A) As good as (C) As far as

(B) As soon as (D) As well as

6. 接続詞と前置詞：They wrote those invoices by hand ------- the serviceperson finished fixing the copier.

(A) by (C) pending

(B) by the time (D) until

7. 接続詞と前置詞：My colleagues were handling customer complaints ------- I was preparing documents for a committee.

(A) among (C) between

(B) while (D) during

8. 接続詞と前置詞：------- Olivia arranged a business trip to Phoenix for our vice president, she had to reschedule it owing to his sudden change of plans.

(A) Though   (C) Despite

(B) However   (D) But

9. 語彙：If you purchase 50 or more items from our stationery and office supplies in a single order, you are entitled to a ------- order discount.

(A) bulk   (C) hulk

(B) folk   (D) talk

10. 語彙：After considerable discussion, we came to the ------- that we should shorten our business hours due to a lack of customers in the early morning and late evening.

(A) confrontation   (C) conclusion

(B) concentration   (D) constitution

解法のポイント 接続詞の問題は選択肢を絞ってから文脈へ

後ろが完全文の節になっている問題では、空所に「接続詞」か「関係副詞」が求められているので、前置詞、接続副詞や関係代名詞などの選択肢はすぐに除外しよう。そのようにして選択肢を絞り込んでから文脈や和訳を考えることで、時間だけでなく、和訳に釣られて誤答を選ぶ危険性も減らすことができる。

Part 7 ターゲット 文章を読むスピードを上げよう

Part 6からPart 7までで読まなければならない文書の量はかなり多いが、試験時間は無制限ではない。最後の問題まで到達するために、とにかく読むスピードを上げる努力をしよう。

Questions 1-4 refer to the following letter.

CheckLink

Dear Mr. Philpot,

This letter is to inform you that you were selected to receive the award for salesperson of the year. Not only have you boosted our company's sales, but you've also patiently scrutinized every complaint from our customers and dedicated your time and energy to identifying problems. — [1] —. Also, to meet customer needs, you've enthusiastically attended different workshops and learned how to handle problems efficiently. All members of your team are always aware from the customer's viewpoint how good our service is. As a result, your team has succeeded in establishing trust and building long-term relationships with each of our customers. — [2] —.

We evaluated your performance and contributions to our company, and have decided to give you the in-house award. — [3] —. This award is the result of your amazing efforts and passion.

At the award ceremony, on July 15th, our CEO Steven Howard will present you with a trophy and reward. We'd like to ask you to give a speech then on behalf of your team. — [4] —.

Sincerely,

Darryl Henning

Darryl Henning, Human Resources Director

1. What is the purpose of the letter?

    (A) To require Mr. Philpot to deal with complaints

    (B) To confirm that all employees will attend workshops

    (C) To ask Mr. Howard to give a brief presentation

    (D) To inform Mr. Philpot that he won an award

2. What is Mr. Philpot's team being praised for?

    (A) Improving the work environment

    (B) Cementing a positive relationship with customers

    (C) Building a magnificent facility for workshops

    (D) Holding the award ceremony on July 15th

3. What is Mr. Philpot asked to do?

    (A) Meet customers

    (B) Increase sales

    (C) Prepare a speech

    (D) Arrange a ceremony

4. In which of the positions marked [1], [2], [3], and [4] does the following sentence best belong?

"Following the ceremony, we will hold a reception to honor you and your great contributions."

    (A) [1]

    (B) [2]

    (C) [3]

    (D) [4]

解法のポイント 語彙力増強は必須

速読のことを語る前に、まず着手すべきなのが語彙力増強だ。当たり前だが、知らない単語が多ければ多いほど、読む速度は遅くなるし、内容にもついて行けなくなってしまう。遠回りに思えるが、読む速さを上げたいなら、語彙力増強は必須だ。

今の大学生にとって必要な*TOEIC*® L&R その勉強をすることの意味とは②

TOEIC® L&Rのための勉強を総合的な英語力につなげる

　TOEIC® L&Rは2時間で200問の問題に挑む、集中力を要するテストです。最初のうちは、問題の音声を十分に聞きとることができずに次の問題が始まってしまったり、読解問題の時間が足りずに終了時間が来てしまったりする受験生もいることでしょう。日常的な場面や不慣れなビジネスに関するかなりの量の英語を聞いて読んで、瞬間的に理解するのは容易なことではありません。そのためには、とにかく英語をたくさん聞いて読んで、地道に練習することが欠かせません。

　こうした*TOEIC*® L&Rのための勉強を続ければ、リスニング・リーディング・語彙・文法のスキルが確実に伸びてきます。*TOEIC*® L&Rのスコアは総合的な英語力を証明するものではありませんので、必ずしも「スコアが高いから英語が堪能」ということにはなりません。しかし、総合的な力の向上には、リスニング・リーディング力や文法の知識、さらに語彙力も絶対に必要で、それらが十分にあるか無いかで、成果の出るスピードに大きな差が出てくるのも事実です。つまり、*TOEIC*® L&Rへの取り組みは、単なる資格や評価の取得にとどまらない、総合的な英語力の土台を育てることにつながるのです。

　単位のため、就職のために*TOEIC*® L&Rの勉強をする、というのが最も分かりやすくてシンプルな理由かもしれません。しかし、英語学習の目的が*TOEIC*® L&Rの高スコアを取ることというのは本末転倒しているようにも思えます。勉強をする過程で培われたリスニングやリーディングの力で、様々な英語のコンテンツにアクセスして楽しむのも良いでしょう。そして、会話力や表現力もアップさせ、実際に外国人とのコミュニケーションに挑戦したり、学生時代に海外旅行や語学研修、留学などに積極的にトライしたりしてみてください。

UNIT 6 Marketing & ICT

Part 1 ターゲット 場所や位置関係に注意しよう

人物や物の位置関係を聞き取ってリスニング問題の正答率を上げよう。

Listen and fill in the blanks for each sentence. Then choose the statement that best describes what you see in the picture.

1.

CheckLink · DL 32 · CD 2-21 ～ CD 2-25

(A) Two men are (　　　　　)
　　(　　　) a (　　　　　　　　).

(B) (　　　　　　) (　　　　　　　)
　　are in (　　　　) of the men.

(C) A man is (　　　　　) (　　)
　　a (　　　　　).

(D) Some (　　　　　　　) are being
　　(　　　　　) from a (　　　).

Choose the statement that best describes what you see in the picture.

2.

CheckLink · DL 33 · CD 2-26

(A)　(B)　(C)　(D)

解法のポイント 前置詞が持つ基本イメージをつかむ

人物や物の位置関係を表すのに使われる前置詞は、英文の後ろの方で読まれる上に、軽く発音されるので聞き取りづらい。また、on、in、at などの前置詞は全て「～で、～に」と和訳されて違いを感じ取ることが難しいので、前置詞を覚えるときには、その前置詞が持つ基本イメージをビジュアル的に習得するとよい。

Part 4 ターゲット 図表付き説明文問題に慣れよう

図表付き説明文問題はPart 4の後半に2題出題される。Part 3と同様、図表はシンプルな予定表、グラフ、クーポン、間取りや地図などなので、焦らず処理しよう。

Listen to the short talk and fill in the blanks. Then choose the best answer to each question. ↻CheckLink 🎧 DL 34 ◎CD 2-27 ~ ◎CD 2-30

This Friday there will be a scheduled (**1.**) (**2.**) and update. The maintenance time is six P.M. to eight P.M. During this (**3.**), no (**4.**) (**5.**) will be (**6.**). So, we ask you to plan your business accordingly. Also, a mandatory (**7.**) session on cyber (**8.**) will be held on Wednesday, (**9.**) tenth. As you (**10.**), unidentified attackers gained (**11.**) to the system of our rival company. They stole its client information (**12.**) several (**13.**) opened suspicious e-mails. We must (**14.**) our company and clients from such attacks. It is (**15.**) to raise staff awareness on cyber security. So, please (**16.**) (**17.**) to (**18.**) the (**19.**) session. You'll be asked to take online courses on cyber security (**20.**) (**21.**) (**22.**) absence.

🎧 DL 35 ◎CD 2-31

1. What is scheduled to happen this Friday?
   (A) A computer system maintenance
   (B) A cyber security training session
   (C) An update of the office building security system
   (D) A relocation of the IT department

2. Why does the speaker say, "So, we ask you to plan your business accordingly"?
   (A) To encourage employees to improve their performance
   (B) To promote staff awareness of cyber security
   (C) To make employees conduct a competitor analysis
   (D) To prepare employees for the server downtime

3. What will the listeners need to do if they miss the event on July 10?
   (A) Talk to their supervisors
   (B) Sign up for online courses
   (C) Cancel the server update
   (D) Click on a link in an e-mail

Listen to the short talk while looking at the graph and choose the best answer to each question. ⟳CheckLink 🎧 DL 36, 37 ⊙CD 2-32 ~ ⊙CD 2-35 ⊙CD 2-36

4. What does the speaker say the business will start?
   (A) Conducting another survey
   (B) Expanding current campaigns
   (C) Creating a new sales promotion
   (D) Releasing the latest model

5. What is mentioned about the Orion Phone?
   (A) It is relatively expensive.
   (B) Many apps are designed for it.
   (C) It is reasonably priced.
   (D) It is the best-selling product.

6. Look at the graphic. According to the speaker, what area requires further analysis?
   (A) Design (B) Ease of operation (C) Features (D) Price

解法のポイント 設問、選択肢、図表の先読みは、やはり必須

Part 3同様、Part 4でも図表問題の3つの設問のうち1つは、"Look at the graphic." で始まる。設問と選択肢をある程度先読みすることが欠かせないということは、すでにUnit 5でも述べたが、Part 4の図表付き説明文問題でも、やはり先読みの時に図表をチェックするのを忘れないこと。

Part 6 ターゲット 文構造を確認しよう

主部が長い文では文構造を見失いがちなので、主語（S）＋述語動詞（V）を常に探すことを心がけよう。

Questions 1-4 refer to the following Webpage. ↻CheckLink

Webinar: Advertising Strategies to Grow E-commerce

Thu. September 5, 8 P.M. – 9 P.M.

This webinar will be presented by Claudia Hilton, CEO of *faceNotebook*, to assist you in creating attractive advertising on social media.

-------. There are tens of millions of users on it, but few can visit your website. The
1.
tips to create a successful website ------- the right targeting, clear pictures,
2.
and the location. In this live session, we will cover how to allow visitors to
reach your website, the proper image size and -------, depending on what you
3.
want to do with your photos, and their best position on the screen. Join our
webinar and use the great opportunity to control your customer base. To
participate, just register on this webpage and get the confirmation e-mail with a
code. You should enter the code and join the seminar ten minutes before the -------
4.
starting time.

Register for the webinar <u>here</u>.

---

1. (A) Your eye-catching online ads have already attracted consumers.

(B) Our advertising department is responsible for the seminar.

(C) Using the Internet makes your shopping experience enjoyable.

(D) The medium is one of the best advertising platforms today.

2. (A) to be

(B) is

(C) are

(D) been

3. (A) resolute

(B) resolution

(C) resoluteness

(D) resolutely

4. (A) above

(B) at

(C) below

(D) into

解法のポイント	まず文構造を確認する癖を付ける

主語が単数形なのに複数を受ける動詞の形を選んでしまった、という単純ミスを避けるためにも、修飾語を取り除いた主語を見抜く力を養ってほしい。

Part 7 ターゲット Triple passage の問題に慣れよう

本問のような５つの設問付きの triple passage 問題は３題出題されるが、割ける時間は３題で21分、１題あたり７分しかない。必要な情報を上手に拾いながら、解き進めよう。

Questions 1-5 refer to the following advertisement, online review, and e-mail.

CheckLink

Marwan the Mover
University Fresher Special

Moving is a stressful experience. Add to that living alone for the first time and starting university, and you have the recipe for a disaster.

Let Marwan the Mover cover your moving needs. Let us reduce your stress with our professional service. Customer satisfaction is guaranteed.

Get online and sign up for our University Fresher Special. Access our smartphone-friendly website, input your details, and mention our promotion campaign to receive the discount. We will reply to you within 24 hours and arrange for your smooth relocation to a new life.

Marwan the Mover × +

◀ ▶ C 🔒 http://www.marwanthemover.biz/

| Home | **Reviews** | Locations | About Us |

Customer Review

Posted by: Stephan Billings **On:** August 20

I just wanted to let you know that your University Fresher Special really helped me out. At this time in my life there is a lot of stress with all the changes that are happening. I really appreciated the specially priced service you provided. All the expenses were piling up and the discount helped me cover other necessities.

I do, however, have to say that I couldn't make the move as scheduled on my first choice of date because the late arrival of your team created some problems. I had been told that the truck would arrive at around 1:30 in the afternoon, but it didn't arrive until about four o'clock. I had been expecting to catch the five o'clock train to the university town, but I had to change my plans at the last moment. It would have been nice to know that there was a delay and the estimated arrival time. Also, only two workers came in, and I think it would have been better if there were more hands.

One other issue was with the browser for the mobile phone. I had trouble inputting information into my account using the browser on my mobile phone. I had to use my friend's laptop to access the site. I recommend you get your software updated soon.

To:	Josh Milligan
From:	Marwan Farquhar
Subject:	Next strategy meeting
Date:	August 29

Josh,

Thanks for all your hard work on the promotion campaign for university students. It has been an outstanding success, maybe too much so. You get all the credit for recommending handing out flyers to graduating high school students.

However, we've also recognized some areas for improvement, so we should hold a strategy meeting. It seems that the pricing was a bit too low. Of course students found it very affordable, but we had a lot of trouble handling all the customers. We rejected some of them because we got too many offers in a short time and failed to make the proper arrangements. Moreover, we couldn't secure enough workers, and we had no choice but to dispatch two workers though we usually dispatch three. Accordingly, some delays occurred. The worst thing is that the profit was very small for the amount of work we put in. By the way, to keep our name in consumers' minds, how about if we announce a thank you for the great response to our promotion? We could also mention our next campaign. Schedule a strategy meeting as soon as possible to look back on this campaign and discuss my idea.

Marwan

1. For whom is the advertisement most likely intended?

(A) High school students of all grades

(B) First-year university students

(C) Graduating university students

(D) Employees of Marwan the Mover

2. What should customers do to receive the discount?

(A) Write a review of the service they received

(B) Sign up for the promotion within 24 hours

(C) Call customer service

(D) Refer to the campaign on the website

3. What problem Mr. Billings mentioned will NOT be discussed at the strategy meeting?

(A) Late arrivals of workers

(B) Trouble with the website

(C) The price of the moving service

(D) Shortage of moving staff

4. What is suggested about Mr. Milligan?

(A) He printed the advertising material.

(B) He resolved the complaints from Mr. Billings.

(C) He was satisfied with the moving cost estimate.

(D) His idea of distributing flyers was appreciated.

5. In the e-mail, the word "affordable" in paragraph 2, line 3, is closest in meaning to

(A) flexible

(B) considerable

(C) reliable

(D) reasonable

解法のポイント 頑張ってみてもダメなら…

Double passage 同様、「①本文の上の枠外にある導入部→②3つの文書それぞれのタイトルや1行目→③設問→④本文」の順番に目を通して時短に努めても、初めの頃はなかなか triple passage の問題の最後までたどり着けないので、*TOEIC*® L&R に不慣れな頃やどうしても時間が足りない人は、この3題丸々15問をひとまず最初にマークしてしまうのも手だ。

Review Test 1

Part

Look at the picture and choose the statement that best describes what you see in the picture.

1.

(A) (B) (C) (D)

2.

(A) (B) (C) (D)

Part 2

Listen to the question or statement and the three responses. Then choose the best response to each question or statement.

3. Mark your answer on your answer sheet. (A) (B) (C)

4. Mark your answer on your answer sheet. (A) (B) (C)

5. Mark your answer on your answer sheet. (A) (B) (C)

6. Mark your answer on your answer sheet. (A) (B) (C)

7. Mark your answer on your answer sheet. (A) (B) (C)

8. Mark your answer on your answer sheet. (A) (B) (C)

Part 3

Listen to the conversations and choose the best answer to each question.

9. Who most likely are the speakers?

(A) Colleagues at a cell phone maker

(B) Mobile phone shop clerks

(C) Customer service representatives

(D) Information Technology engineers

10. What problem are the speakers discussing?

(A) They had to pay a lot for a marketing team.

(B) The sales figures did not increase as much as expected.

(C) They could not launch a promotional campaign in New York.

(D) They cannot help increasing the price of the product.

11. What will the speakers do next?

(A) Consider the strategies of the competitor

(B) Have a sales meeting before lunch

(C) Collect and analyze data

(D) Continue the discussion after a lunch break

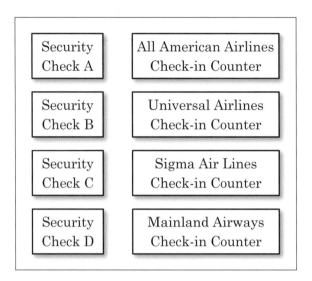

12. Where is the conversation taking place?

    (A) At the boarding gate

    (B) At the check-in counter

    (C) At the baggage claim area

    (D) At the security checkpoint

13. What does the man ask the woman to do?

    (A) Change his seat

    (B) Book a window seat

    (C) Pick up his baggage

    (D) Proceed to the boarding gate

14. Look at the graphic. Which airline is the man flying with?

    (A) All American Airlines

    (B) Universal Airlines

    (C) Sigma Air Lines

    (D) Mainland Airways

Part 4

Listen to the short talks and choose the best answer to each question.

15. What is the main topic of the talk?

(A) Emergency exit routes

(B) Community support services

(C) Information security

(D) Preparation for disasters

16. Why does the speaker say, "you should consider what to do about your pets"?

(A) The listeners cannot bring their pets.

(B) Animals can be good companions.

(C) The listeners may evacuate with their pets.

(D) Pet owners should obey public rules.

17. What does the speaker remind the listeners to do during an emergency?

(A) Copy ID papers and certificates

(B) Help others who need assistance

(C) Make decisions quickly

(D) Persuade neighbors to evacuate

Culture and Art Tour Itinerary		
Time	**Location**	**Must-see**
10:30 A.M. – 12:00 P.M.	Natural History Museum	Skeleton of T-Rex
1:00 P.M. – 2:30 P.M.	Nielsen Gallery	Miniature Art
2:30 P.M. – 4:00 P.M.	Contemporary Art Museum	3D-printed Sculptures
4:00 P.M. – 5:30 P.M.	Metropolitan Gallery	Abstract Paintings

18. What is mentioned about the Nielsen Gallery?

(A) It is being renovated.

(B) It is holding a special exhibit.

(C) It is closed today.

(D) It features Impressionist paintings.

19. Look at the graphic. When will listeners most likely attend the curator's talk?

(A) 10:30 A.M. – 12:00 P.M.

(B) 1:00 P.M. – 2:30 P.M.

(C) 2:30 P.M. – 4:00 P.M.

(D) 4:00 P.M. – 5:30 P.M.

20. According to the speaker, how can listeners receive a discount at the gallery shop?

(A) By asking for a group discount

(B) By showing the tour ticket

(C) By buying exclusive items

(D) By paying in cash

Part 5

Choose the best answer to complete the sentence.

21. My first ------- of the sales representative was rather good, and she seemed calm, generous and reliable.

(A) impress   (B) impressive   (C) impressively   (D) impression

22. The CEO of Southern Airlines ------- the possibility of decreasing the number of their shuttles running to and from the airport.

(A) mentioned   (C) has mentioned about
(B) was mentioned by   (D) had mentioned of

23. Information about our big promotion campaign can be shared among all of ------- through the cloud-based system.

(A) we   (B) our   (C) us   (D) ourselves

24. Our new 10-week course by Peter Hopkins is intended for ------- interested in effective fund-raising methods.

(A) either   (B) those   (C) which   (D) them

25. The release date for the film has been postponed ------- because one of the cast members was arrested.

(A) define   (B) indefinite   (C) indefinitely   (D) definition

26. ------- Best Sell Appliance provides same-day installation of refrigerators, an additional fee will be charged.

(A) Though   (B) However   (C) Despite   (D) Nevertheless

27. Last Saturday a real estate agent took us to view an apartment, which is located ------- walking distance of Penn Station and Casey's Department Store.

(A) into   (B) while   (C) altogether   (D) within

28. In case Jack can't come back due to the cancellation of all flights, either you or Michael ------- to make a presentation instead of him.

(A) are going   (B) were supposed   (C) has   (D) will likely

Part 6

CheckLink

Questions 29-32 refer to the following information.

Warm Weather Shipping Policy

At Chocolate Factory, we take great care in creating our delicate chocolate

------- heat destroys chocolate. -------. Therefore, we specially package and
  29.   **30.**

ship your gift so that it will be delivered in perfect condition.

When temperatures reach 70 degrees Fahrenheit or higher at the delivery

destination, we strongly recommend ------- the insulated shipping option.
                                                      31.

We ------- suggest deciding a delivery date when someone can accept your
   32.

order and put it into the refrigerator right away. Insulated packaging with frozen

gel packs and delivery on an appointed date require additional charges. If you fail

to choose this option and your order melts, we cannot be held responsible.

---

29. (A) besides

    (B) due to

    (C) although

    (D) because

30. (A) It seems quite difficult to melt
        chocolate perfectly.

    (B) We would like to explain our
        manufacturing strategies.

    (C) We want you to have chocolate
        with the best taste, texture and
        appearance.

    (D) This is why our products include
        the damaged chocolate.

31. (A) to choose

    (B) chose

    (C) choose

    (D) choosing

32. (A) sometime

    (B) reluctantly

    (C) also

    (D) soon

Part 7

Questions 33-35 refer to the following letter.

David Jackson
50 6th Ave.
Tacoma, WA 98406

Dear Mr. Jackson,

We would like to invite you to attend the taste-test dinner, which will be held at our headquarters in Seattle, on July 5 at 6 P.M. This event is intended to show our accomplishments and to have the opportunity of obtaining your feedback. If you can join us, let us know before June 20 by phone. We will send an invitation card with details immediately. You will be paid, and your travel expenses will be reimbursed.

The procedure for the day is as follows: when you arrive at our office building, show your invitation card at reception and sign in. You will then be taken to the dinner venue. Before starting dinner, you will fill out a form with the necessary information. After the meal, you will complete a survey and submit it.

Please keep in mind that our building is currently under construction. Therefore, if you come by car, you can park it in the parking lot in the Sports Center, located across from our establishment.

Please be aware of our non-disclosure policy. You cannot disclose any information about the event, including what you ate and what questions you were asked.

You have always cooperated with our survey, and we hope you will help us again.

Sincerely,

Andrew O'Donnell
Andrew O'Donnell
Director of Marketing
Mars Foods Company

33. What is the purpose of the letter?

    (A) To give notice of renovations

    (B) To announce a new policy

    (C) To advertise the latest products

    (D) To extend an invitation

34. What is indicated about Mars Foods Company?

    (A) Its parking area is currently unavailable.

    (B) It has a large number of employees.

    (C) It has launched kitchen utensils.

    (D) Its headquarters has been rebuilt.

35. What is suggested about Mr. Jackson?

    (A) He will apply for a parking permit.

    (B) He has taken part in the project before.

    (C) He will pay for his meals.

    (D) He is Mr. O'Donnell's subordinate.

Questions 36-40 refer to the following e-mail and invoice.

To:	smorris@landtoland.net
From:	jeremybolston@housesnmore.ca
Subject:	Condo Renovations
Date:	April 23

Hi, Sabrina.

How have you been? It's been a while.

I'm writing because I need your advice. I recently bought a piece of property. Initially I thought it was quite reasonable. However, after examining it more closely, there are many repairs that need to be made. I've remodeled homes before, but this condo is a lot more work than I anticipated. I've already had several parts remodeled recently, but to bring this place up-to-date I will need to invest more time and money than expected. I don't know if I will be able to get a return on my investment. Additional fees are starting to add up, too. Also, I want the renovations to be done by the end of June because, from July, I'll be out of town on business for two months.

Fortunately, thanks to regular inspection and maintenance, the overall quality and condition of the building is good. I met some of the other tenants the other day and they seem to be quite friendly and helpful.

You've had experience with condo renovations, right? Do you think you could spare a couple of hours this week to visit the place? I would really appreciate your feedback. We could then go for lunch at a nice restaurant I found. It's just around the corner.

Looking forward to hearing from you and catching up.

Best regards,
Jeremy Bolston

INVOICE

Azure Construction

2597 Fillini Ave.
Middleland, MI
836-7835

Invoice Number: #A00254
Issue Date: June 15
Due Date: July 5

Bill to:

Jeremy Bolston
184 Polestar St., Apt. 503
Middleland, MI
875-2309

Details	Amount	Price
Waste disposal	2 tons	$585
Plumbing	28 hours	$1,764
Electricity	9 hours	$468
Kitchen remodeling	35 hours	$1,960
Kitchen installation	1 unit	$16,850
	Sub-total	$21,627
	State tax (9%)	$1,946
	Total	$23,573
	Deposit	$2,800
	Payment Due	**$20,773**

Note: There is a 6-month guarantee on the workmanship as of the issue date of
this invoice. Kitchen equipment has a 5-year warranty.

36. What is the problem with the condo Mr. Bolston bought?

(A) It was more expensive than he thought.

(B) It needs a lot of repairs.

(C) The neighbors are unsociable.

(D) There are no eating establishments nearby.

37. What does Mr. Bolston ask Sabrina to do?

(A) To advise him by e-mail

(B) To invest money in the building

(C) To visit his condo

(D) To begin the renovation process

38. What is most likely true about the renovation work?

(A) It was finished before Mr. Bolston left for his business trip.

(B) It did not include plumbing work.

(C) It cost more than the estimate.

(D) It was carried out under the supervision of Sabrina.

39. What is indicated about Mr. Bolston?

(A) He sees Sabrina almost every day at the office.

(B) He has renovated many apartments and condos before.

(C) He hired a local company for the renovations.

(D) He likes quaint old residences.

40. How much did it cost Mr. Bolston to renovate his condo before taxes?

(A) $2,800

(B) $20,773

(C) $21,627

(D) $23,573

Production & Logistics

Part 1 ターゲット 言い換えに注意しよう

Part 1では「言い換え」がよく使われる。簡単な語句で表すことができるものが、難しい単語や、抽象的な表現で言い換えられたりするので、柔軟に対応しよう。

Listen and fill in the blanks for each sentence. Then choose the statement that best describes what you see in the picture.

1.

CheckLink DL 38 CD 2-43 ~ CD 2-47

(A) (　　　　　　) are (　　　　　　)
　　(　　　　　　　　) headgear.
(B) The road (　　　) (　　　　)
　　(　　　　) with asphalt.
(C) A (　　　　　) is being put up
　　(　　　　　) the (　　　　　　)
　　lot.
(D) (　　　　　) are (　　　　　　)
　　heavy (　　　　　　　　　)
　　machinery.

Choose the statement that best describes what you see in the picture.

2.

CheckLink DL 39 CD 2-48

(A)　(B)　(C)　(D)

解法のポイント 自分の語彙に縛られた予想はしない

例えば写真に自動車が写っているとする。carという単語が読み上げられると予想する人が多いだろうが、実際にはautomobile「自動車」やvehicle「車両」という単語が流れてくることが多い。また、タブレット型端末が写っていてtabletという単語が読み上げられると予想していると、electronic device「電子機器」という語句が聞こえてきたりする。このように難しい単語や抽象的な表現で言い換えられていると、一瞬反応が遅れてしまうので、Part 1では自分の語彙に縛られた予想は立てずに、音声に受け身になった方がよい。

Part 2 　ターゲット　助動詞のイディオムを確認しよう

Could you ~?や Would you ~?などの助動詞を使った表現は、形式上は疑問文であるが、「～できましたか」「～するつもりですか」の意味ではなく、「～していただけませんか」という依頼の意味で用いられることが多い。Part 2やPart 3で頻出の、助動詞のイディオムをまとめてチェックしよう。

Listen and fill in the blanks for each sentence. Then choose the best response to each question or statement. ⟳CheckLink 🔽 DL 40 ~ 42 ◎ CD 2-49

◎ CD 2-50 ~ ◎ CD 2-53

1. (　　　　　) (　　　　　) (　　　) put the list of sample materials?
(A) The list (　　　) (　　　) (　　　) longer.
(B) (　　　　　　) (　　　　　　) 1 and 2 P.M.
(C) (　　　　) (　　　) (　　　) (　　　) to Greg?

◎ CD 2-54 ~ ◎ CD 2-57

2. (　　　　) (　　　) (　　　) (　　　) to estimate the cost for the durability test?
(A) That would (　　　) (　　) (　　) (　　).
(B) After the test (　　　　) (　　　) (　　).
(C) Yes, (　　) (　　).

◎ CD 2-58 ~ ◎ CD 2-61

3. _____ the developers return?
(A) _____ at six.
(B) I'm sorry, _____ now.
(C) Yes, _____ the R&D section now.

Listen to the question or statement and the three responses. Then choose the best response.

4. (A)　(B)　(C) ⟳CheckLink 🔽 DL 43 ◎ CD 2-62

解法のポイント　応答表現も併せて要チェック

〈依頼〉や〈申し出〉に対する応答は、受け入れるか断るかのどちらかの場合が多い。「～してくれませんか」という〈依頼〉に対して、受け入れる場合は "OK." "Sure." "No problem." などで応答し、断る場合は "I'm sorry I can't." や "Maybe later." などで応答する。また「～しましょうか」という〈申し出〉に対して、受け入れる場合は "Yes, please." や "That would be great." などで応答し、断る場合は "No, thank you." や "I'm fine, thanks." などで応答する。いずれの応答表現もパターン化されているので、併せて確認しておくと大変効果的だ。

Part 5 　ターゲット　助動詞をマスターしよう

Choose the best answer to complete the sentence. 　 CheckLink

1. 助動詞の用法：Manufacturers and construction companies must ------- of industrial waste properly and safely in accordance with municipal regulations.

(A) dispose (C) disposed

(B) disposes (D) disposing

2. 助動詞の意味：Thanks to the increase in plant capacity, Spencer Synthetics Co. ------- produce two and a half times as many chemical compounds as before.

(A) must not (C) would often

(B) can (D) are going to

3. 助動詞＋助動詞：If traditional retailers don't adapt to polarization in consumption patterns, they ------- survive.

(A) won't can (C) won't be able to

(B) can will not (D) can be not going to

4. 助動詞＋過去の表現：The researchers in the R&D division of P&B Chemipharma Ltd. must ------- out many experiments patiently until they were able to create that innovative artificial placenta.

(A) carry (C) be carried

(B) carried (D) have carried

5. 仮定法現在：The US Department of Labor demands that every construction worker ------- a protective helmet or hardhat.

(A) wear (C) wore

(B) wearing (D) worn

6. イディオム：We built the condo according to the working drawing, so we ------- help feeling there was something wrong with the architect's blueprint.

(A) couldn't (C) wouldn't

(B) shouldn't (D) didn't

7. **イディオム**：Though you ------- well pursue productivity and profit, you must take care of your talented staff who are valuable assets.

(A) will

(C) may

(B) can

(D) should

8. **イディオム**：I would ------- operate a machine or work on an assembly line than monitor a production process.

(A) prefer

(C) quite

(B) instead

(D) rather

9. **語彙**：We have been using the ------- company for many years to deliver our containers from the dock to our warehouse.

(A) physics

(C) logistics

(B) statistics

(D) pediatrics

10. **語彙**：General Technologies' factories have undergone several random ------- since the new facility safety standard was implemented.

(A) interpretations

(C) infections

(B) inspections

(D) innovations

解法のポイント **助動詞のイディオム習得はリスニング問題に有効**

近年のPart 5では、助動詞に関しては、助動詞の意味を問う問題や仮定法現在を問う問題などが出題されているものの、出題回数自体は減っている。だが、それでもやはり助動詞のイディオムはPart 2やPart 3で頻出なので、リスニングパートでの高得点獲得のために早めの攻略がおススメだ。

オンラインチャットやテキストメッセージ形式の問題は、読む分量も比較的少なく、また会話文に近いため、口語調で、語彙も特殊なものや難解なものは少ない。全部読んでも大した時間のロスにはならないので、設問を先読みした後に最初から順に全文を読んで、流れを把握しながら読み解こう。

Questions 1-4 refer to the following online chat discussion.

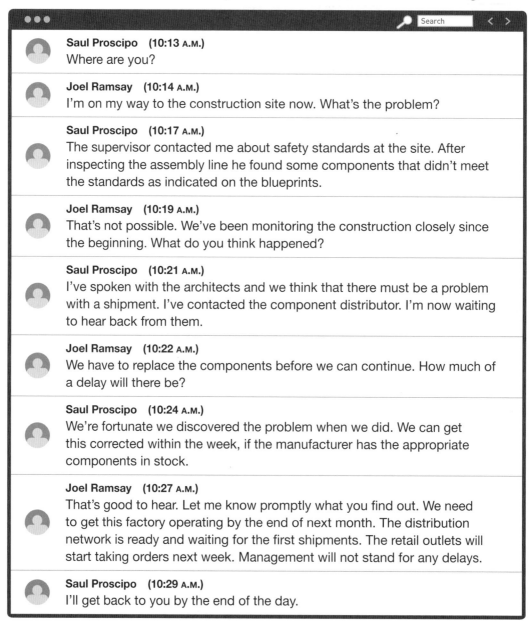

Saul Proscipo (10:13 A.M.)
Where are you?

Joel Ramsay (10:14 A.M.)
I'm on my way to the construction site now. What's the problem?

Saul Proscipo (10:17 A.M.)
The supervisor contacted me about safety standards at the site. After inspecting the assembly line he found some components that didn't meet the standards as indicated on the blueprints.

Joel Ramsay (10:19 A.M.)
That's not possible. We've been monitoring the construction closely since the beginning. What do you think happened?

Saul Proscipo (10:21 A.M.)
I've spoken with the architects and we think that there must be a problem with a shipment. I've contacted the component distributor. I'm now waiting to hear back from them.

Joel Ramsay (10:22 A.M.)
We have to replace the components before we can continue. How much of a delay will there be?

Saul Proscipo (10:24 A.M.)
We're fortunate we discovered the problem when we did. We can get this corrected within the week, if the manufacturer has the appropriate components in stock.

Joel Ramsay (10:27 A.M.)
That's good to hear. Let me know promptly what you find out. We need to get this factory operating by the end of next month. The distribution network is ready and waiting for the first shipments. The retail outlets will start taking orders next week. Management will not stand for any delays.

Saul Proscipo (10:29 A.M.)
I'll get back to you by the end of the day.

1. What is suggested about Mr. Proscipo?

(A) He has never been to the construction site.

(B) He is working on the assembly line in the component plant.

(C) He is not satisfied with the safety standards.

(D) He was informed that some parts were not good enough.

2. At 10:19 A.M., what does Mr. Ramsay most likely mean when he writes, "That's not possible"?

(A) It is not true that the supervisor inspected the assembly line.

(B) It is hardly possible that he will visit the construction site soon.

(C) There is no way that defective components could be found.

(D) He does not believe that the safety standards are being met.

3. Why is Mr. Ramsay concerned?

(A) Mr. Proscipo was not able to contact the distributor.

(B) It takes time to replace the deficient parts.

(C) The architects did not find out about the problem.

(D) The appropriate components are out of stock.

4. When is the factory planning to start operating?

(A) Within the week

(B) Next week

(C) By the end of next month

(D) By the end of the day

解法のポイント 複数人物のやりとりに慣れる

「文字化された会話文」を読み慣れると、解答のスピードも正答率もさらにアップする。インターネットで英語の掲示板などを見たりして、会話の形式やそこで使用される英語の表現に接する機会を増やそう。

Employment

Part 1　　ターゲット　写真上に現れる、進行形と完了形の違いを学ぼう

Part 1では、現在形や現在進行形だけでなく、現在完了形も頻繁に用いられている。時制の違いがもたらす写真の違いを認識しよう。

Listen and fill in the blanks for each sentence. Then choose the statement that best describes what you see in the picture.

1. 　　🔄CheckLink　🎧 DL 44　◎CD 2-63 ～ ◎CD 2-67

(A) Some chairs have (　　　　　)

(　　　　　　　　) in a (　　　　　　).

(B) The people (　　　) (　　　　　　)

some (　　　　　　　　).

(C) A woman (　　) (　　　　　　) (　　　)

a form.

(D) The (　　　　) are (　　　　　　)

(　　　　　　　　) the wall.

Choose the statement that best describes what you see in the picture.

2.　　🔄CheckLink　🎧 DL 45　◎CD 2-68

(A)　(B)　(C)　(D)

解法のポイント　現在完了形は動作の完了後、現在進行形は動作の最中

現在完了形の和訳は「～した」で、現在進行形の和訳は「～している」だが、写真ではこの2つは決定的な違いとなって現れる。現在完了形はすでに動作が終わっている状態を、現在進行形は動作が行われている最中を表す。例えば "Chairs have been stacked." なら、写真には積み上がった椅子が写っている。一方、"Chairs are being stacked." なら、今まさに積み上げ作業の真っ最中なので、写真には椅子を積み上げている人物が写っているはずだ。

Part 3 ターゲット 会話の全体的な流れをつかもう

受験者が会話を全体的に把握できているかどうかを試すために、「何が話されているのか」を問う設問は頻繁に出題される。Part 3のほとんどが2人の会話であり、3人の会話は少ないが、登場人物が増えたからといって焦ってはいけない。2人の会話でも3人の会話でも、「話題」をきっちりつかんで、話の流れにうまく乗ろう。

Listen to the conversation and fill in the blanks. Then choose the best answer to each question. ↻CheckLink 🎧 DL 46 ⊙CD 2-69 ～ ⊙CD 2-74

M: Hello, Ms. Standridge. I'm Denis Bryant. I (1.   ) (2.   )
(3.   ) forward to (4.   ) you.

W: Welcome. Please have a seat. After this (5.   ), the department
(6.   ) will meet you. We only have forty-five minutes, so let's
(7.   ) (8.   ). You (9.   ) (10.   ) Sunrise IT Systems.
How long have you been there?

M: (11.   ) years. I have ten years of experience in designing and developing a
(12.   ) (13.   ) (14.   ) systems and networks there.

W: I see. I notice from your (15.   ) that you worked on
(16.   ) (17.   ). What was your most
(18.   ) accomplishment?

M: I worked as a (19.   ) (20.   ) to develop a new information
system three years ago. It took two full years, but the administration
(21.   ) and office management system have (22.   )
drastically.

🎧 DL 47 ⊙CD 2-75

1. Why has the woman started the interview quickly?
   (A) Another interview is scheduled.
   (B) The room will be unavailable.
   (C) A department meeting will be held.
   (D) The managers will leave the office.

2. How many years of work experience does the man have?
   (A) At least 2 years   (C) At least 5 years
   (B) At least 3 years   (D) At least 10 years

3. What was the man's job?
   (A) Actor   (B) Engineer   (C) Architect   (D) Proofreader

83

Listen to the conversation and choose the best answer to each question.

CheckLink DL 48, 49 CD 2-76 ~ CD 2-81 CD 2-82

4. What do the speakers say recently happened?

(A) Cindy left the company for personal reasons.

(B) Daniela got a position as a senior editor.

(C) Mr. Martinez quit the company.

(D) The man replaced Mr. Martinez.

5. What does the woman imply when she says, "So what will become of us"?

(A) She wants to start a new project soon.

(B) She is anxious about the staff shortage.

(C) She is looking forward to a new article.

(D) She intends to apply for the position.

6. Where do the speakers most likely work?

(A) At a pharmaceutical company

(B) At a temp agency

(C) At a publisher

(D) At a computer manufacturing plant

解法のポイント 会話のシチュエーションと人物の関係性に注意

Part 3は、男性1人と女性1人、男性2人と女性1人、女性2人と男性1人のいずれかの組み合わせ
で、ビジネスシーンや日常生活での会話が展開される。どのようなシチュエーションで、どのような
関係にある人物たちが、何の話をしているのかを意識しながら、会話文を聞き取ろう。

Part 6 ターゲット 話の流れから時制を読み取ろう

Part 5同様、動詞の活用が問われている場合、時制が関係していることが多い。ただし、短文穴埋め問題として出題されるPart 5とは違って、長文穴埋め問題であるPart 6では文脈が大事なので、空所が含まれる英文だけでなく、前後の英文まで広く観察して時制を読み取ろう。

Questions 1-4 refer to the following e-mail.

ⒸCheckLink

From: Susan Wilkinson
To: Chris Goldman
Date: 19 April
Subject: Job offer from Wilkinson, Bello & Gibson LLP

Dear Mr. Goldman,

We are delighted to offer you the position of senior associate with an

anticipated start date of the first of June. Please find attached the terms and

------- of your employment. If you choose to accept this offer, we would like to
　1.
have your ------- by 29 April.
　　　2.

In addition, we are holding our 30th anniversary ceremony on 13 May. It will

be a good opportunity for you to socialize with your new colleagues before

starting work with us. We ------- transportation and accommodation and all
　　　3.
expenses are covered. To make arrangements for them, we have to check

how many people will be coming. -------.
　　　　4.

In the meantime, please don't hesitate to reach out to me, either through

e-mail or by calling me directly at 7227-2525, if you should have any

questions or concerns. We are looking forward to hearing from you and hope

you'll join our team!

Best regards,

Susan Wilkinson
Wilkinson, Bello & Gibson LLP

1. (A) recommendations
   (B) conditions
   (C) guidelines
   (D) allowances

2. (A) response
   (B) respond
   (C) respondent
   (D) responder

3. (A) are arranged
   (B) to arrange
   (C) will arrange
   (D) arranging

4. (A) A vegan diet will be available.
   (B) The shuttle bus is expected to arrive on time.
   (C) Please let us know of your attendance by the date above.
   (D) Complimentary refreshments will be served to the staff.

解法のポイント 時間・文構造の次は、流れを意識する

Unit 2では「時間」に留意して、Unit 6では「文構造」に注意して解く癖をつけるようアドバイスした。それが自然にできるようになったら、次は *TOEIC*® L&R の問題はもちろんのこと、それ以外の英文にもたくさん触れて、流れと展開をつかむ「読解力」を磨いてほしい。

Part 7 ターゲット 求人広告に慣れよう

求人広告には、業務内容の他、応募要件、待遇、応募にあたっての注意事項などが書かれている。広告なので、文脈を意識して文章を読むよりも、情報を整理しながら求められている人物像を的確につかんだ方がよい。

Questions 1-4 refer to the following job advertisement.

CheckLink

Job Opening

Employer : C&C Media
Location : London with regular international travel
Industry : Media, Advertising, Marketing & PR
Job title : Advertising Sales Executive
Salary : Strong base salary plus commission
Hours : Full time
Contract : Permanent
Job level : Executive

Job Description:
We are in search of a highly motivated advertising sales executive to join our growing team. The jobholder will be responsible for driving international advertising sales and developing new business opportunities.

Main Duties:
- Maintain and expand relationships with current clients
- Maximize existing revenue potential
- Develop new areas of advertising by acquiring new clients

Qualifications:
- Minimum of five years of advertising sales experience at a senior level
- Bachelor's degree in advertising, marketing, business, or related majors required; master's degree preferred
- Advanced knowledge of online advertising sales
- Ability to communicate effectively with international clients
- Fluency in Spanish not required but desirable
- Strong math and analytical skills

Apply online at **www.cc.media.com/workhere**
or send your CV to **jobs@cc.media.com**

NOTE: Please do not ask referees to send us any letters; these will be requested by us for final candidates only.

1. What will be the main responsibility of the successful candidate?
   (A) Developing profitable products
   (B) Expanding advertising business
   (C) Setting up international branch offices
   (D) Reforming the company structure

2. What qualification or skill is necessary in applying for this position?
   (A) A bachelor's degree in job-related majors
   (B) A master's degree in linguistics
   (C) Experience in a multinational environment
   (D) Fluency in Spanish

3. What is indicated about this position?
   (A) It requires travelling abroad.
   (B) It is fully commission based.
   (C) It requires experience as a sales representative.
   (D) It is suitable for a new graduate.

4. The word "referees" in Note, line 1, is closest in meaning to
   (A) relatives
   (B) colleagues
   (C) judges
   (D) supporters

解法のポイント 求められている人物像を絞り込もう

求人広告には、部署名や職位名だけでなく、資格や学位を示す略号（BA、BS、MA、MBA、MS、PhD
など）も出てくるので、関連語彙を強化しておこう。また、応募者に求められる必要条件と十分条件
を区別して、ターゲットとなる人物像を正確に把握すること。"ideal" や "desirable" は「あれば有利な
条件」を示し、"required" は「必須条件」を意味している。

UNIT 9 Personnel

受動態

Part 1 　ターゲット　受動態の表現に慣れよう

受動態の文はPart 1の選択肢でよく使われている。現在形の受動態（is [are] + 過去分詞）だけでなく、been や being と絡む受動態の文に慣れよう。

Listen and fill in the blanks for each sentence. Then choose the statement that best describes what you see in the picture.

1. CheckLink　DL 50　CD 2-83 ~ CD 2-87

(A) A cardboard box (　　) (　　　　　　)
　　 (　　　　　　).

(B) They (　　　) (　　　)
　　 (　　　　　　　) suits.

(C) A brick pillar (　　) (　　　　　)
　　 (　　　　　).

(D) Some (　　　　　) (　　　　)
　　 (　　　　　　) to a woman.

Choose the statement that best describes what you see in the picture.

2. CheckLink　DL 51　CD 2-88

(A)　(B)　(C)　(D)

解法のポイント　現在完了形や現在進行形と受動態が絡む形に注意

現在完了形の受動態（have [has] been + 過去分詞）や、現在進行形の受動態（is [are] being + 過去分詞）といった、been や being が絡む受動態がよく聞き取れないという声は少なくないが、毎回当たり前のように出題されており、避けて通れないので、早いうちに慣れたいところだ。

Part 4 ターゲット オフィスやビジネス関連の用語に慣れよう

オフィスやビジネスの場面での発話は、社会経験のない学生にとっては、なじみの薄いものである。しかし、あらかじめ会社の部署名や役職名、ビジネス関連の用語を知っておくと、状況を想像しやすくなる。語彙を増やすことで、自分が経験したことのない状況での発話にも対応できるようにしておこう。

Listen to the short talk and fill in the blanks. Then choose the best answer to each question. CheckLink DL 52 CD 2-89 ~ CD 2-92

Hello, everyone, I'm Maria Lopez, administrative manager. I'm delighted to
(1.   ) the (2.   ) of Daniel Tanaka as the
new marketing (3.   ). Daniel joined our company (4.   )
years ago and has (5.   ) (6.   ) roles in
both (7.   ) management and (8.   ). During his time
in the product management team, his ideas helped to (9.   ) the
(10.   ) competitiveness of our products. His (11.   )
(12.   ) was highly (13.   ) by the company's
(14.   ), Patrick Lipinski. As the new marketing director, Daniel is going to
(15.   ) a (16.   ) (17.   ) to (18.   ) new markets
in Southeast Asia. He will also take over the (19.   ) project
with Nelson and Noble initiated by the present director, Carlos Cabrera. As you
know, Carlos is retiring in two months' time. Now, please (20.   ) (21.   ) in
congratulating Daniel and wishing him every (22.   ) in his new position.

DL 53 CD 2-93

1. What is the main purpose of this speech?

(A) To announce a promotion

(B) To advertise a job vacancy

(C) To honor a retiring employee

(D) To accept an award

2. According to the speaker, who is leaving the company in a few months?

(A) Maria Lopez (C) Patrick Lipinski

(B) Daniel Tanaka (D) Carlos Cabrera

3. What does the speaker ask the listeners to do for Mr. Tanaka?

(A) Toast his health (C) Acknowledge him as their CEO

(B) Give him their good wishes (D) Appoint him to be a new director

Listen to the short talk and choose the best answer to each question.

CheckLink DL 54, 55 CD 2-94 ~ CD 2-97 CD 2-98

4. Where most likely is the talk being made?

(A) At a board meeting

(C) At a job interview

(B) At a reception

(D) At an orientation session

5. What are the listeners asked to do when entering the building?

(A) Use temporary keys

(C) Scan their badges

(B) Wear company uniforms

(D) Show their IDs

6. What are the listeners going to do next?

(A) See a demonstration

(C) Listen to a speech

(B) Watch a video

(D) Hold a welcome party

解法のポイント Part 4 も導入部を逃さない

"Questions xx through xx refer to the following" に続く箇所に announcement が入れば「空港や駅などでのアナウンス」や「社内でのお知らせ」、telephone message なら「留守番電話」、advertisement なら「広告」、excerpt from a meeting なら「会議の抜粋」、talk なら「博物館や施設のツアーガイドの話」や「スピーチ」、news report や broadcast なら「ニュース」などとなる。ジャンルが分かっているだけでも心の準備がしやすくなるので、集中してこの導入部を聞き取ってほしい。

Part 5 ターゲット 受動態をマスターしよう

Choose the best answer to complete the sentence.

CheckLink

1. 基本用法：The resignation letter I had submitted last month ------- by the human resources manager yesterday.

(A) formally accepted

(C) have been formally accepting

(B) has formally accepted

(D) was formally accepted

2. 紛らわしい動詞：Your tax rate rises as your salary -------, so your net income won't increase as much as you expect.

(A) rise　　(B) is raised　　(C) will be risen　　(D) have raised

3. 紛らわしい動詞：Ms. Wang ------- to a senior manager above her immediate boss since her performance was highly evaluated.

(A) is promoting

(C) was promoted

(B) has promoted

(D) had been promoting

4. 助動詞＋受動態：If you are entitled to a housing allowance, that amount can ------- in different ways depending on what type of property you live in.

(A) pay　　(B) is paid　　(C) have paid　　(D) be paid

5. 完了形＋受動態：Though Mr. Hodgins ------- to training new recruits for years, he will be transferred to a subsidiary as of April 1.

(A) commits　　　　　　(C) has been committed

(B) was committing　　(D) had committed

6. by以外が続く受動態：Our general manager became interested ------- the new project I planned and proposed, and I was appointed as a project leader.

(A) in　　(B) on　　(C) with　　(D) by

7. 句動詞の受動態：The proposed merger of Woodman Furniture and Franklin Furnishing was ------- the CEO of Franklin Furnishing's parent company.

(A) called off　　(B) called off by　　(C) called by　　(D) called by off

8. 句動詞の受動態：Enrique was injured in the car accident and has to be hospitalized for two months, so his duties will be ------- some of his colleagues.

(A) take over　　(B) taken over　　(C) taken by over　　(D) taken over by

9. 語彙：The vice president and his ------- are going to visit and inspect their overseas branches next month.

(A) subordinates　　(B) subscriptions　　(C) submissions　　(D) subcontracts

10. 語彙：The supervisor ------- Louise to replace her former coworker who was in charge of the big promotion campaign with the sales department.

(A) made　　(B) persuaded　　(C) had　　(D) let

解法のポイント 基本から応用まではすぐそこ！

受動態は、基本形を少し発展させるだけですぐ応用問題が解けるようになる項目だ。まず、by以外の前置詞を使う表現を覚え、次に、助動詞、不定詞や動名詞、様々な時制と組み合わせると、どういう形になるかを確認しよう。それほど問題のバリエーションも多くなく、比較的理解しやすいところなので、ぜひ攻略してほしい。

スキャニング (scanning) とは、文章全体を「探して見渡す (scan)」ことで、大量の文章から特定の情報を探し出す、いわゆる「拾い読み」「探し読み」のことだ。スキャニングを上手に利用して、速読に生かそう。

Questions 1-5 refer to the following letter and schedule.

◯ CheckLink

Kerry Robertson
38 Thompson Street
Green Village, California 58977
209-334-9272, ext.42
robertson@southernpacific.com

May 24

Nolan Miller
42 Washington Street
North Valley, California 57766

Dear Mr. Miller:

We are excited that you have decided to accept our offer of employment. I would like to welcome you to our company on behalf of all the staff. Your first day of the induction program is Monday, June 3. We will expect you at 9:00 A.M. The first day is full of meetings and opportunities. You will meet people with whom you will work closely, and I am sure you can successfully integrate into your new department.

First, you will meet your new supervisor, or mentor, Stacy White. She plans to describe your new job broadly and provide details of your orientation. After meeting her, you will attend an orientation about company policy and other important matters.

I have enclosed the schedule, a map of the office and facilities, a copy of the company brochure, and documents for new employees. Please don't forget to bring them and also your SSN and driver's license as well.

Again, it is our pleasure to welcome you to Southern Pacific Trading Corporation. If you have questions, or need additional information prior to your start date, please feel free to call me at any time, or send me an e-mail. We look forward to working with you soon.

Best regards,
Kerry Robertson
Kerry Robertson
HR Manager, Southern Pacific Trading Corporation

Induction Program Schedule
— Day 1 —

Time	Room	Activities
9:00 A.M. - 10:00 A.M.	Room 201	▸ Meet your new supervisor ▸ Overview of your new role and details of orientation
10:00 A.M. - 11:00 A.M.	Room 202	▸ Welcome video ▸ Presentation on company policy, structure, and office regulations by staff of HR department
11:00 A.M. - 11:30 A.M.		▸ A tour of the office
11:30 A.M. - 12:00 P.M.	Room 312	▸ Meet managers and your department colleagues
12:00 P.M. - 1:30 P.M.	Cafeteria	▸ Lunch with your new team
1:30 P.M. - 3:30 P.M.	Room 501	▸ Learn the details of your department and job
3:30 P.M. - 4:30 P.M.	Room 202	▸ Complete new-hire paperwork

Note: The ID you receive at orientation must be worn at all times. Coffee, snacks and lunch are provided.

1. What is the purpose of the letter?

    (A) To arrange an HR department meeting

    (B) To inform Mr. Miller of interview results

    (C) To give information on the induction program

    (D) To explain the company policy

2. In the letter, the phrase "integrate into" in paragraph 1, line 6, is closest in meaning to

    (A) conflict with

    (B) depend on

    (C) interfere with

    (D) mix with

3. Where should Mr. Miller go to meet Ms. White?

    (A) Room 201

    (B) Room 202

    (C) Room 312

    (D) Room 501

4. What is NOT mentioned about items to bring?

    (A) Lunch

    (B) Paperwork

    (C) A map

    (D) The company brochure

5. When will Mr. Miller learn about the specifics of his work duties?

    (A) 10:00 A.M.-12:00 P.M.

    (B) 12:00 P.M.-1:30 P.M.

    (C) 1:30 P.M.-3:30 P.M.

    (D) 3:30 P.M.-4:30 P.M.

解法のポイント 設問を先に読み、キーワードを探す

先に設問を読んで何が問われているかを確認したら、必要な情報のターゲットを絞り、該当箇所を探し出す。関連するキーワードが必ず本文にあるので、そのキーワードを中心に読み進め、文書の内容から選択肢をよく吟味して解答しよう。究極のやり方として、そのキーワードの周辺のみを読み拾っていくという方法もあるが、もちろんこれは追い込まれた時の最終手段なので、普段は真面目に練習しよう。

Part**1** ターゲット -ing 形の用法を確認しよう

Part 1では動詞の-ing形が頻繁に登場するが、このユニットでは-ing形の異なる用法に留意して写真問題に取り組もう。

Listen and fill in the blanks for each sentence. Then choose the statement that best describes what you see in the picture.

1. CheckLink DL 56 CD 3-01 ~ CD 3-05

(A) They are (   ) the
(   ).

(B) They are (   ) at the
(   ) (   ).

(C) They are (   ) the (   )
(   ).

(D) They are (   ) on
(   ).

Choose the statement that best describes what you see in the picture.

2. CheckLink DL 57 CD 3-06

(A)   (B)   (C)   (D)

解法のポイント 現在進行形か現在分詞の限定用法か

Part 1では、動詞の-ing形は現在進行形（be動詞 + -ing）の形で用いられることがほとんどだが、a sitting woman「座っている女性」やa man trimming trees「木を剪定している男性」のように、-ingが名詞の前後に付いてその名詞を修飾する「現在分詞の限定用法」の場合もある。

Part 2　ターゲット　変則的な応答問題に注意しよう

Part 2では、ほとんどの問題が「疑問文＋平叙文」のやりとりで構成されているが、「平叙文＋平叙文」や「平叙文＋疑問文」、「疑問文＋疑問文」のように変則的なやりとりの構成もある。

Listen and fill in the blanks for each sentence. Then choose the best response to each question or statement. ⟲CheckLink 🎧 DL 58～60 ◎CD 3-07
◎CD 3-08 ～ ◎CD 3-11

1. I'll describe the (　　　　) of our business partnership (　) (　　　　)
(　　　).
　(A) We (　　　) (　　) (　　　　) (　) a new place.
　(B) The proposed (　　　　　) (　　　) (　) (　　　　)
　　　abandoned.
　(C) Thanks, but I think (　) (　　) (　　　　) (　).

◎CD 3-12 ～ ◎CD 3-15

2. Frankly speaking, there seems to be (　) (　　　) for
(　　　　　　).
　(A) (　　　　　), I'm (　　) (　　　　).
　(B) Do you think we (　　　　) (　　　) (　) the plan?
　(C) Frank (　　　) (　　　) (　　　　　) his strategy.

◎CD 3-16 ～ ◎CD 3-19

3. I heard _____ for the next
fiscal year.
　(A) The new _____ their competitors.
　(B) The _____
　　　accepted.
　(C) That's _____?

Listen to the question or statement and the three responses. Then choose the best response.

4. (A)　(B)　(C) ⟲CheckLink 🎧 DL 61 ◎CD 3-20

解法のポイント　変則的な問題には柔軟性が大事

例えば、同僚が「コピー機が壊れているよ」と言った場合、①「本当に？困るなぁ」という感想、②「2週間前に点検してもらわなかった？」という質問、③「業者に連絡して来てもらおう」という提案のいずれも、応答として自然である。尋ねられたことにただ答える「疑問文＋平叙文」の問題とは違って、変則的な問題の応答文はバリエーションが多いので、選択肢を一つずつ当てはめながら状況を想像して、最も自然なやり取りが成立するものを選ぼう。

Part 5 ターゲット 分詞と分詞構文をマスターしよう

Choose the best answer to complete the sentence. CheckLink

1. 限定用法：The enterprise promised an improvement of hospitality programs for their shareholders because of their ------- stock price.
(A) skyrocket
(C) skyrocketed
(B) skyrocketing
(D) being skyrocketed

2. 限定用法：Argos Industries consulted an attorney about a patent ------- by a competitor, and they are carefully preparing to file a lawsuit.
(A) infringe   (B) infringing   (C) infringed   (D) infringes

3. 物事の性質：The news that negotiations over the merger and acquisition with K-Mobile had completely broken down was ------- to our management.
(A) disappointed
(C) to disappoint
(B) disappointing
(D) disappointment

4. 人の感情：Our management was ------- at the news that negotiations over the merger and acquisition with K-Mobile had completely broken down.
(A) disappointed
(C) to disappoint
(B) disappointing
(D) disappointment

5. 分詞構文：MT Express Co. and Trucker Road Ltd. held a joint press conference, ------- a strategic business partnership to collaborate in the field of logistics networking.
(A) announcer
(C) to be announced
(B) announcing
(D) announcement

6. 分詞構文： ------- with the second quarter of the previous year, the sales and profits of the Internet mail-order corporation increased substantially in the same quarter of this year.
(A) Compare   (B) Comparing   (C) Comparison   (D) Compared

7. 分詞構文：------- from some key economic indicators, the economy is highly likely to have emerged from a long period of recession.

(A) Judging   (B) Judgement   (C) Judged   (D) Judgmental

8. 付帯状況：Their president, frowning with his arms -------, listened to a proposal from a business consultant on strategy for the next decade.

(A) to fold   (B) fold   (C) folding   (D) folded

9. 語彙：------- has allowed new firms to enter the market, reduced monopolies, and promoted competition.

(A) Irregular   (B) Regularly   (C) Deregulation   (D) Regulate

10. 語彙：In order to build community and enhance their business processes, entrepreneurs today should ------- advantage of every available tool, including the Internet and social media.

(A) avail   (B) make   (C) take   (D) use

解法のポイント 分詞構文の問題では常に「主語」を意識する

分詞構文の問題で空所の前に名詞がない場合、分詞構文の意味上の主語と主節の主語は一致する。------- from a distance, the hotel looks like a castle. という問題の場合、空所前に名詞がないので、主語は主節の the hotel と同じということだ。ホテルには「目」が付いてないので、「見る側」か「見られる側」では、「見られる側」に決まっている。したがって正解は Seen となる。

企業や業界、市場の動向についてレポートした経済記事は、出題頻度が高いものの、大学生にはやや
ハードルが高く感じられるかもしれない。普段から日本語や英語の経済ニュースに目を通し、扱われ
ている内容や、よく使われる用語とその意味を押さえておこう。

Questions 1-4 refer to the following article.

ⓒCheckLink

Lincolnshire Business Report

Gainsborough, September 19 – Healthful Pharmaceuticals is a leading national drug company. In the last couple of years they have launched several successful supplements onto the market. The company has become quite prosperous following the deregulation of over-the-counter drug sales. Investors have been anticipating some big news from the company in the last few months.

Healthful Pharmaceuticals held a press conference today to announce their partnership with Anak Pharmaceuticals of Indonesia. Director Trent Farnsworth explained to reporters that the company has made this decision in order to gain access to the Southeast Asian market, which is expected to be the next big growth area for pharmaceuticals. The expanding middle class, along with steady economic growth, has led the firm to make the decision to go full speed ahead into this market. This partnership will help them to establish a presence in the Asian region. Mr. Farnsworth told reporters, "We see this as a stepping stone into the larger Asian market. Our plan is to increase our market share by making use of both the local human resources and the abundant natural resources."

The official signing of the partnership will be held at the headquarters of Anak Pharmaceuticals in Jakarta on September 21. The construction of a new factory in Indonesia will begin in October, with completion expected in July next year. The factory will be in full operation a month after that.

1. How has Healthful Pharmaceuticals become successful?

    (A) It has sold supplements in local markets.

    (B) It has benefited from the deregulation of drugs.

    (C) It has launched new businesses.

    (D) It has made an announcement to their investors.

2. According to the article, where is the area with great potential for
pharmaceuticals?

    (A) Lincolnshire

    (B) Gainsborough

    (C) Southeast Asia

    (D) The Middle East

3. What will Healthful Pharmaceuticals do with Anak Pharmaceuticals?

    (A) Conserve natural resources

    (B) Develop new drugs

    (C) Encourage the economic growth of Indonesia

    (D) Gain a larger share of the Asian market

4. When will the construction of a new factory finish?

    (A) This September

    (B) This October

    (C) Next July

    (D) Next August

解法のポイント 設問からキーワードを見つける

先に設問に目を通し、その中からキーワードを見極めよう。特に設問中の固有名詞は必ずチェックしよう。キーワードを手がかりに本文を読むことで、解答に必要な部分を効率よく読むことができる。ただし、本文中ではキーワードが別の表現に言い換えられていることもあるので要注意。

Health & Environment

不定詞・動名詞

Part 1 　ターゲット　専門用語に慣れよう

TOEIC® L&Rテストは、日常生活やビジネスシーンで使用される英語を中心に構成されているが、医療や環境などのやや専門性の高い話題が登場することもある。出題される頻度はそれほど高くないが、高得点を目指す人はぜひとも押さえておきたいところだ。

Listen and fill in the blanks for each sentence. Then choose the statement that best describes what you see in the picture.

1.
   CheckLink 　 DL 62 　 CD 3-21 ～ CD 3-25

(A) A (　　　　) station is (　　　　　　)
    (　　　　　　　　　　).
(B) (　　　　　　　　) (　　　　　　　　)
    are being (　　　　　　　).
(C) Smoke is (　　　　　　) up from a
    (　　　　　　) (　　　　　　　　).
(D) (　　　　　　　　　　) are
    (　　　　　　　　) the plant
    (　　　　　　　　　　　).

Choose the statement that best describes what you see in the picture.

2.
   CheckLink 　 DL 63 　 CD 3-26

(A)　(B)　(C)　(D)

解法のポイント 　幅広く英文に触れる機会を増やす

逆説的ではあるが、*TOEIC®* L&R対策テキスト以外で日頃からどれだけ多くの英語に触れているかが高得点への近道だ。新聞、雑誌、書籍、ウェブなどあらゆる媒体の多様な英語にたくさん触れるようにしよう。日本国内のニュースを英語で配信しているメディアから始めると、元ネタが分かっているので内容を理解しやすく、あまり抵抗なく読み進められるだろう。

Part 3　ターゲット　話し手が暗示する意図や示唆するものを探ろう

Part 3 の 3 つの設問は、①会話全体の流れや話題を問うもの、②「いつ」「どこで」「誰が」「何を」「なぜ」「どのように」したのか／するのかといった会話の詳細を問うもの、③話し手が暗示する意図や示唆するものを問うものの、3 つのパターンに分けられる。③については、話し手が直接言及していないことも多いため①や②よりも難しいかもしれないが、会話全体を理解した上でその流れから意図や示唆するものを見極め、適切な解答を選びたい。

Listen to the conversation and fill in the blanks. Then choose the best answer to each question. ⟲CheckLink 🎧 DL 64　◉ CD 3-27 ～ ◉ CD 3-31

M: Did you (1.　　　　) the recent e-mail sent to all employees by the

(2.　　　　　　)?　He says we must (3.　　　) CO_2 levels before the

(4.　　　　　　　) of our facilities next year.

W: A three (5.　　　　　) (6.　　　　　　　) will do (7.　　) (8.　　　　　)

(9.　　) comply with new (10.　　　　　　　　　), but he insists that we

should reduce emissions by five percent.

M: (11.　　　　) (12.　　　　　　　) special (13.　　　　　　　) in new

technology, though we can improve our corporate value by promoting the fact that

we are a company that has consideration for the (14.　　　　　　　　).

W: People are becoming (15.　　　　) (16.　　　　) (17.　　　　) aware of the need

to (18.　　　) the (19.　　　　　　) (20.　　　　　　) the environment

and the economy. We'll be regarded as one of the best (21.　　　　　　)

(22.　　　　　) companies, which can greatly benefit our business.

🎧 DL 65　◉ CD 3-32

1. What did the president recently do?

(A) He inspected the facilities.

(B) He announced his resignation.

(C) He sent an e-mail to his staff.

(D) He reduced CO_2 emissions.

2. What does the woman imply when she says, "he insists that we should reduce emissions by five percent"?

(A) The goal is rather difficult to meet.

(B) New regulations need to be tightened.

(C) The facilities should be inspected soon.

(D) Investment amounts have been cut.

3. How will the company probably be perceived?

    (A) As a globally competitive company

    (B) As a well-known plant and flower company

    (C) As an environmentally friendly company

    (D) As a successful solar energy company

Listen to the conversation while looking at the floor plan and choose the best answer to each question. ⟳CheckLink 🎧DL 66, 67　◎CD 3-33 ~ ◎CD 3-37　◎CD 3-38

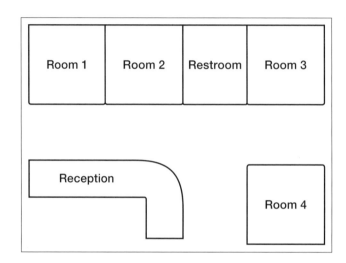

4. Where most likely are the speakers?

    (A) In an airport　　　　　　　　(C) In a garage

    (B) In an examination room　　　(D) In a pharmacy

5. What problem does the woman mention?

    (A) She has heavy luggage on her back.　(C) She cannot find a pharmacy.

    (B) She feels chilly when sleeping.　　　(D) She has been sick recently.

6. Look at the graphic. Where is the woman directed to go?

    (A) Room 1　　(B) Room 2　　(C) Room 3　　(D) Room 4

解法のポイント 会話の文脈を把握して、論理的に考える

話し手の意図や示唆するものを問う設問は、Why does the speaker [man, woman] say, "~"? や What does the speaker [man, woman] mean [imply] when he [she] says, "~"? という聞き方をされる。なぜ、あるいはどんな意図で話し手がそのような発言をしているのか、発言の前後の文脈を理解し、因果関係をよく考えて解答したい。

Part 5 ターゲット 不定詞・動名詞をマスターしよう

Choose the best answer to complete the sentence. ⟳CheckLink

1. 名詞的用法：Governor Paul Howell, advocating sustainable energy, promised ------- the district's own municipal regulations of carbon dioxide emissions.

  (A) set   (C) to set

  (B) setting   (D) to being set

2. 形式主語と不定詞・動名詞：It is important to stop ------- all supplements and vitamins, as well as medicines that contain iron, for a week before a colonoscopy.

  (A) take   (C) to take

  (B) taking   (D) taken

3. 不定詞・動名詞：Water authorities investigated the contamination of drinking water and warned residents that toxic substances needed ------- from the water.

  (A) eliminate   (C) to eliminate

  (B) eliminating   (D) eliminated

4. 疑問詞に続くとき：The poster on the bulletin board of our community center says when and where ------- out the unburnable trash.

  (A) take   (C) to take

  (B) taking   (D) taken

5. 原型不定詞：Clarice had a dentist thoroughly ------- her teeth, gums, jaw, and bite for the first time in a while thanks to her full coverage health insurance.

  (A) check   (C) to check

  (B) checking   (D) checked

6. 結果・程度：Most of the residents opposed the incinerator construction because it could pollute the environment, but the mayor pushed the plan ------- to construct it.

  (A) so force as   (C) too forcibility

  (B) enough forcible   (D) forcibly enough

7. 目的：Vincent submitted a medical certificate and decided to take two weeks of sick leave ------- to worsen his symptoms.

(A) so as not   (C) in case

(B) such as   (D) not in order

8. 慣用表現：The city council discussed whether to charge for an ambulance to prevent citizens ------- one improperly.

(A) called   (C) to call

(B) calling   (D) from calling

9. 語彙：Researchers in the ------- company are repeating experiments day after day to develop a new drug with no side effects.

(A) philosophical   (C) phenomenal

(B) pharmaceutical   (D) physiological

10. 語彙：The physician wrote a ------- for cough and fever medicine to the patient suffering from a cold.

(A) ascription   (C) prescription

(B) description   (D) subscription

解法のポイント 目的語が不定詞か動名詞かで意味が違う他動詞に注意

目的語が不定詞か動名詞かで意味の異なる他動詞の場合、不定詞は「まだ起こっていない事柄」や「これから行う行為」を、動名詞は「既に起こった事柄」や「既に行った行為」を表すという違いがある。

a) I forgot to buy copy paper.

b) I forgot buying copy paper.

a)は「私はコピー用紙を買うのを忘れた」という意味でコピー用紙は未購入、b)は「私はコピー用紙を買ったことを忘れていた」という意味でコピー用紙は購入済みということになる。

Part 7　ターゲット　時間配分を体で覚えよう

Part 7はテンポよく解いていくことが求められる。英文をゆっくりと熟読する癖がついている人は、「速く解く」ことを常に念頭に置いて取り組もう。

Questions 1-4 refer to the following notice.　　　　　CheckLink

New Rules for Garbage Collection

Starting on January 10th, the new rules for garbage collection will take effect. —[1] —.

● Collection days will be changed: burnable trash will be collected every Tuesday and Friday; non-burnable trash every Wednesday; and cans and bottles (plastic ones included) every Thursday.

● Cardboard will be collected on the 2nd and 4th Monday from a designated container near the one for burnable trash, which means it should no longer be categorized as burnable trash. — [2] —.

● Although plastic containers for food items such as butter, yogurt, or cooking oil were allowed to be put into garbage bags for plastic trash under the old rules, these kinds of trash will be newly categorized as "plastic containers for food items" and should be thrown away in newly designated bags every Wednesday. — [3] —. The bags will be sold in every supermarket and convenience store in this city.

These new rules were set because the mayor aims at making our city one of the top eco-friendly cities. — [4] —. We are very sorry for taking up too much time and effort of the people of this city, but thank you for your understanding and cooperation.

1. Who is the notice intended for?

    (A) The mayor

    (B) Sanitation workers

    (C) Local residents

    (D) Protesters

2. What is indicated about the new rules?

    (A) They were rejected by the mayor.

    (B) They require citizens to separate waste in detail.

    (C) They will charge the citizens for littering.

    (D) They were set on January 10th.

3. According to the new rules, when should a plastic bottle for cooking oil be thrown away?

    (A) The 2nd and 4th Monday

    (B) Every Tuesday

    (C) Every Wednesday

    (D) Every Thursday

4. In which of the positions marked [1], [2], [3], and [4] does the following sentence best belong?

"She and the city council have worked together very hard to establish these new rules."

    (A) [1]

    (B) [2]

    (C) [3]

    (D) [4]

解法のポイント 自分の解答時間を計測する

感覚的に速く解いている「つもり」を防ぐために、ストップウォッチで解答時間を正確に計測してみよう。思ったよりも時間がかかっている苦手な形式や、設定時間よりも早く解答できる得意な形式など、自分の傾向が分かってくるので、そこから対策を練っていこう。

UNIT 12 Finance

Part 1　ターゲット　同音異義語や、品詞で意味の異なる語に注意しよう

Part 1では音声面での「ひっかけ」で、同音異義語や品詞で意味が異なる語などが出題されるので、注意しよう。

Listen and fill in the blanks for each sentence. Then choose the statement that best describes what you see in the picture.

1.  CheckLink　DL 68　CD 3-39 ~ CD 3-43

　(A) She's (　　　　　　　) (　　　)
　　　(　　　　　) of a machine.
　(B) She's (　　　　　　) (　　　　) a
　　　(　　　　　　　　).
　(C) She's (　　　　　　) her (　　　　　　)
　　　(　　　　　).
　(D) She's (　　　　　　　) (　　　　) a
　　　(　　　　　).

Choose the statement that best describes what you see in the picture.

2. CheckLink　DL 69　CD 3-44

(A)　(B)　(C)　(D)

解法のポイント　音だけでなく、内容も考慮する

He'sはHe isの短縮形でもありHe hasの短縮形でもある上に、所有格のhisと音が似ている。またplaceは名詞では「場所」の意味だが、動詞では「〜を置く」の意味である。このような紛らわしい語も、音だけでなく文の意味を考えれば、適切に判断することができるようになる。

Part 4 ターゲット 数字を含む説明文に慣れよう

数値や時間、日付など、数字が含まれる説明文は多い。しかし、数字そのものは、説明の中でデータの一つとして触れられているに過ぎない場合もある。数字だけにフォーカスし過ぎず、具体的な数字を用いてどういった現象や動向が説明されているのかを聞き取ろう。

Listen to the short talk and fill in the blanks. Then choose the best answer to each question. CheckLink DL 70 CD 3-45 ~ CD 3-48

I'll talk about (1.) (2.) to keep your eyes on. This week I'm watching a company called Smart Loan. It's a provider of on-line (3.) services. Today, it is a growing presence in the mortgage and (4.) (5.) markets. (6.) the (7.) (8.) years, the entire mortgage industry has benefited from the housing boom with low (9.) (10.). Now, interest rates have been raised again, and mortgage applications (11.) (12.) (13.) (14.). However, investors remain optimistic about Smart Loan's prospects. We can see its strong (15.), (16.) (17.) its development of innovative digital mortgage technology. (18.), I own Smart Loan shares myself, and I'm (19.) as to how well it will (20.) the change in situation. I'll (21.) to (22.) its progress.

DL 71 CD 3-49

1. What is the talk mainly about?

(A) An interesting property   (C) A loan payment

(B) A notable business   (D) An annual report

2. What does the speaker mean when she says, "investors remain optimistic about Smart Loan's prospects"?

(A) Investors believe Smart Loan will continue to grow.

(B) Smart Loan is confident about providing bargain-priced properties.

(C) High interest rates will seriously affect Smart Loan.

(D) Mortgage and real estate stocks will be stable.

3. What does the speaker say she will continue to do?

(A) Sell Smart Loan shares

(B) Watch Smart Loan's stock prices

(C) Sign up for Smart Loan's services

(D) Apply for a mortgage through Smart Loan

Listen to the short talk while looking at the chart and choose the best answer to each question. ⟲CheckLink ⬇ DL 72, 73 ◉CD 3-50 ~ ◉CD 3-53 ◉CD 3-54

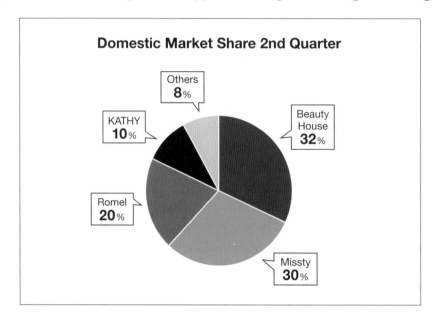

4. According to the speaker, what happened to the speaker's business in the second quarter?

(A) Its profits improved in one division.

(B) It achieved its highest operating income.

(C) It appointed a new leader.

(D) It went through a merger.

5. Who is Richard Bowers?

(A) An executive   (C) An auditor

(B) An accountant   (D) A bank clerk

6. Look at the graphic. What percent of the market did the speaker's business hold in the second quarter?

(A) 32%   (B) 30%   (C) 20%   (D) 10%

解法のポイント 集中力と頭の切り替えが大切

TOEIC® L&R では、メモを取ることができない。リスニングセクションでは聞いている最中に意識が他に行ってしまわないよう、集中力を保つことが大切。同様に大切なのが、一つの問題にこだわらず、すばやく注意を切り替えること。分からない問題を考え続けていると、次の問題が聞き取れず解答できないという、負の連鎖が起きてしまう。くれぐれも前の問題は引きずらないで、今取り組んでいる問題に集中しよう。

Part 6 　ターゲット　文挿入問題を攻略しよう

文挿入問題はPart 7のsingle passageの問題にも出題されるが、Part 7は空所が各パラグラフに散りばめられていることが多く、それぞれのパラグラフに解法の手がかりが点在している。それに対してPart 6の文挿入問題は、決められた空所に最も適切な文を選ぶ形式なので、手がかりは空所の前後に限られている。手がかりが少ない分、Part 6の文挿入問題の方が、Part 7の文挿入問題よりも難易度は高いというわけだ。唯一の手掛かりとなる空所の前後の文をしっかり確認したい。

Questions 1-4 refer to the following article.　　　　　　　　　ⒸCheckLink

---

Gabbard Electronics to Restart Plants

Beijing (May 15)—A spokesperson for Gabbard Electronics, ------- is based in
　　　　　　　　　　　　　　　　　　　　　　　　　　　　　　1.
Guangzhou, has confirmed that all five domestic plants will ------- their
　　　　　　　　　　　　　　　　　　　　　　　　　　　　　　　2.
production of liquid crystal displays, or LCDs, next month. In an effort to
accommodate a downturn in demand from Asian countries, the ------- halted
　　　　　　　　　　　　　　　　　　　　　　　　　　　　　　3.
manufacturing its products in those plants for up to two months. During the
plant shutdowns salaries have been paid to workers so employee confusion
was kept to a minimum. -------. The major factor behind poor performance
　　　　　　　　　　　　4.
was less demand from Asians, especially from the Japanese. It might be
difficult for them to keep operating all plants in the near future unless the
company looks for a feasible and effective solution.

1. (A) what

   (B) where

   (C) which

   (D) when

2. (A) resume

   (B) open

   (C) finish

   (D) expose

3. (A) organizer

   (B) organized

   (C) organization

   (D) organize

4. (A) Employees would try to negotiate for a rise in salary.

   (B) He decided to revise the company policy.

   (C) Management might not be optimistic, though.

   (D) The personnel department will be closed for the time being.

解法のポイント	代名詞と時制に注意

文挿入問題の正解の選択肢に代名詞が使われている場合、空所までの文中に、その代名詞を指す名詞があるはずだ。また、文書全体の内容や時間の流れを正確につかめていれば、空所に挿入する文の正しい時制も予想できる。空所の前後に出てくる単語にばかり気を取られずに、代名詞や時制に注目しながら選択肢を絞りこむこと。

Part 7 ターゲット スキミングをマスターしよう

スキミング（skimming）とは、文章の要点を「すくい取る（skim）」ことで全体の大まかな意味をつかむ、いわゆる「斜め読み」「流し読み」のことだ。スキミングを上手に利用して、速読に生かそう。

Questions 1-5 refer to the following Webpage and e-mails. CheckLink

| Home | **News** | Locations | About Us |

Starcorp Bank Mobile Banking
Banking at your fingertips

1. Convenient transactions, anytime, anywhere!
Various banking functions, and more, available on your mobile phone.

2. Easy Login!
Use biometric authentication and log in immediately.

Functions
➢ balance inquiry
➢ itemized deposit and withdrawal inquiry
➢ bank transfer
➢ tax and utility payment options
➢ reset cash card PIN number
➢ debit card / credit card item inquiry
➢ point inquiry

Click here and get the app!

Mortgage Refinancing Campaign

For the duration of the campaign, administrative fees have been waived. That's right, $0 to refinance your mortgage. Don't miss this chance.
Click here for refinancing simulation.

Notes:
● Applying for refinancing must be completed at one of our branches.
● It may be necessary to submit additional forms to complete the application process.
● Refinancing is not guaranteed.

To:	inquiry@starcorpbank.com
From:	Joe Kishikawa <jkishikawa@ffm.com>
Subject:	Refinancing
Date:	Monday, October 14, 0:19 A.M.

Hello,

I downloaded the application. At approximately 11 P.M. on October 13 I tried accessing my account but got an error message. What should I do now?

Also, I heard from my friend Mike Singleton, who refinanced his mortgage with you, that he was able to save $140 a month on payments and about $33,000 on his overall mortgage. I'd like to schedule an appointment to discuss what could be done about my mortgage. What documents do I need to bring along? The nearest location from my place is the Clifton branch.

Joe Kishikawa

To:	Joe Kishikawa <jkishikawa@ffm.com>
From:	Glenn Redford <redford@starcorpbank.com>
Subject:	Re: Refinancing
Date:	Monday, October 14, 11:15 A.M.

Dear Mr. Kishikawa,

I apologize for the problem you encountered accessing the mobile site. Please note that the site cannot be accessed due to regular system maintenance from Sunday 9:00 P.M. to Monday 7:00 A.M. Also, when the site is extra busy, it may be difficult to log in. In that case, please wait a moment and try again.

Thank you for considering refinancing your mortgage. To determine refinancing eligibility, we require a preliminary review of your current mortgage. Please bring some ID, a statement of annual income, the property deeds, and the mortgage documents. The mortgage officer at Clifton is Roy Chang. We ask that you make an appointment in advance by phone. We look forward to your visit.

Glenn Redford
Customer Service
Starcorp Bank

1. What is the purpose of the webpage?

   (A) To announce a new policy   (C) To advertise a mobile phone

   (B) To provide information   (D) To explain payment at a bank

2. What are the users of Starcorp Bank's mobile banking NOT able to do on their mobiles?

   (A) Confirm a balance   (C) Open a new account

   (B) Pay a utility bill   (D) Log in with a fingerprint

3. What is suggested about Mr. Singleton?

   (A) He is a representative of Starcorp Bank.

   (B) He paid the additional fee to refinance his mortgage.

   (C) He previously worked closely with Mr. Redford.

   (D) He has been to a Starcorp Bank branch.

4. Why did Mr. Kishikawa have trouble logging in?

   (A) He entered the wrong passwords.

   (B) The bank stopped the service temporarily.

   (C) The website had heavy access from users.

   (D) His mobile phone did not work properly.

5. In the second e-mail, the word "preliminary" in paragraph 2, line 2, is closest in meaning to

   (A) simplified   (C) severe

   (B) complicated   (D) provisional

解法のポイント 設問タイプで解き方を変える

本文を読む前に設問に目を通しておくと、スキャニングしながら「人名」「時間」「場所」などの問われている情報を見つけることに集中できる。一方、What is indicated [suggested / implied] ~?「~について何が示されていますか［分かりますか／示唆されていますか］」などの、選択肢が文になっている、全体の内容について問われる設問は、スキャニングだけで解答を出すことは難しい。このような選択肢照合型設問の場合は、本文全体をスキミングし、そこで得た情報を集約させて解答を出さなければならない。究極のスキミング法として、それぞれの段落の最初と最後の文だけ読むという方法もあるが、もちろんこれは追い込まれたときの最終手段なので、普段は真面目に練習しよう。

Review Test 2

Part

Look at the picture and choose the statement that best describes what you see in the picture.

1.

(A) (B) (C) (D)

2.

(A) (B) (C) (D)

Part 2

Listen to the question or statement and the three responses. Then choose the best response to each question or statement.

3. Mark your answer on your answer sheet. (A) (B) (C)
4. Mark your answer on your answer sheet. (A) (B) (C)
5. Mark your answer on your answer sheet. (A) (B) (C)
6. Mark your answer on your answer sheet. (A) (B) (C)
7. Mark your answer on your answer sheet. (A) (B) (C)
8. Mark your answer on your answer sheet. (A) (B) (C)

 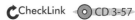

Part 3

Listen to the conversations and choose the best answer to each question.

9. What is the conversation mainly about?
   (A) Entrepreneur seminars
   (B) Environmental protection
   (C) Personnel changes
   (D) Community development

10. What made the woman decide to stay in Seattle?
    (A) She is going to launch a joint project with a local company.
    (B) Her boss stopped her from transferring to headquarters.
    (C) She prefers to stay in her hometown.
    (D) She loves the business culture and environment of Seattle.

11. What is suggested about Bradley?
    (A) He does not want to leave Seattle.
    (B) He was dissatisfied with his routine job.
    (C) He could not find a job in Los Angeles.
    (D) He has a complaint about his boss.

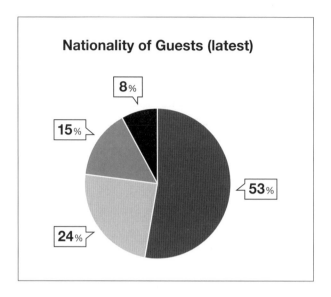

Nationality of Guests (latest)

8%
15%
53%
24%

12. In which industry are the speakers working?

(A) Hospitality

(B) Financial services

(C) Transportation

(D) Construction

13. Look at the graphic. What percentage of guests do the Japanese account for?

(A) 53%

(B) 24%

(C) 15%

(D) 8%

14. What reasons does the woman give for the number of Japanese guests decreasing?

(A) Geographical reasons

(B) Cultural reasons

(C) Political reasons

(D) Economic reasons

Part 4

Listen to the short talks and choose the best answer to each question.

15. Why does the speaker say, "Do you have a clear plan for a successful product launch"?

(A) To offer some effective ideas

(B) To ask for marketing support

(C) To develop new products

(D) To invite the listeners to an event

16. What kind of service is being advertised?

(A) Telephone installation work

(B) Computer user support

(C) Overnight shipping

(D) Public relations

17. According to the speaker, what is available free of charge?

(A) A telephone consultation

(B) A PR campaign

(C) A marketing service

(D) A product sample

	Basic Accounts	Simple Accounts	Super Accounts	Smart Accounts
Price	$15.00	$18.00	$30.00	$18.00
Release date	May 10	April 15	May 1	April 1

18. What is the main topic of the talk?

(A) Product information

(B) Financial analysis

(C) Accounting reports

(D) Technical instructions

19. Who will be interested in the talk?

(A) TV reporters

(B) Customer service representatives

(C) Business owners

(D) App developers

20. Look at the graphic. When will the product the speaker recommends for beginners become available?

(A) May 10　　(B) April 15　　(C) May 1　　(D) April 1

Part 5

Choose the best answer to complete the sentence.

21. All workers ------- safety shoes and goggles in the automobile assembly plant as outlined in their safety manual.

(A) will be worn   (B) must wear   (C) can be wearing   (D) should be worn

22. The state-of-the-art surveillance camera set up at the back door showed clearly how the thief ------- into the office the night before.

(A) will break   (B) breaks   (C) has broken   (D) had broken

23. Since a larger space was required, the head office of Beaute Cosmetics ------- to Oxnard in California five years ago.

(A) relocates   (C) was relocated

(B) is relocating   (D) has been relocated

24. The residents ------- concern that the construction of the proposed apartment complex will cause traffic jams conducted a protest demonstration in front of the city hall.

(A) expressing   (C) who were expressed

(B) express   (D) having been expressed

25. ------- from very durable materials, our sheds are strong enough to hold up to three feet of snow accumulation on their roofs.

(A) Make   (B) Made   (C) Making   (D) For making

26. Staff members accompanying our area manager on store visits are allowed ------- straight home on those days.

(A) go   (B) goes   (C) going   (D) to go

27. The management recalled Mr. Taylor, the outstanding executive candidate ------- had turned the struggling London branch around.

(A) what   (B) which   (C) who   (D) whose

28. Ms. McFarlane went to Star Trust Bank the other day, ------- the teller recommended that she get a biometric bank card.

(A) when   (B) which   (C) wherever   (D) what

CheckLink

Part 6

Questions 29-32 refer to the following advertisement.

Whether you need lawn maintenance, removal of tree debris, or installment of a

pergola, Arden Landscape will ------- all your expectations.
29.

Arden Landscape was ------- by Martine Arden in 2000. We have since been
30.
providing a ------- range of services: design, landscape and maintenance. We
31.
mainly serve residential and commercial clients in Essex, UK.

We are committed to providing a perfect solution for our clients. We speak

with them to ensure that their requirements will be met at every stage. We are

also committed to creating the perfect garden. -------. From consultation to
32.
completion, we will provide turnkey services.

29. (A) see
   (B) require
   (C) stand
   (D) meet

30. (A) establish
   (B) established
   (C) establishing
   (D) to establish

31. (A) comprehend
   (B) comprehension
   (C) comprehensive
   (D) comprehensively

32. (A) They are expected to attend our
      workshop.
   (B) We work closely with experienced
      garden architects.
   (C) We sell tools for gardening at reduced
      prices.
   (D) We extend our business hours during
      the peak seasons.

Part 7

Questions 33-35 refer to the following letter.

Chris Johnson
23 West 25th Street #506
Bronx, NY 10471
Telephone: 212-367-0942

15 October

Ms. Alice Burnett
Systems Engineering Manager
MET Microsystems
33 East 4th Street
New York, NY 10003

Dear Ms. Burnett,

It was a pleasure meeting you on Monday. I appreciated the opportunity to talk with you and your associates in person regarding the systems engineer position.

Our meeting increased my interest and enthusiasm for working for MET Microsystems. The position seems quite challenging and I am impressed by your systems engineering team, hoping to become part of it. I am confident that my 10 years of work experience as a systems engineer satisfies the job requirements. With my experience and skills, I would be able to contribute significantly to your company.

Thank you again for the opportunity to learn more about your organization. Please let me know if I can provide you with any additional information. If you have any questions, please contact me at 212-367-0942 or cjohnson@ frontier.com. I look forward to hearing from you.

Sincerely yours,

Chris Johnson
Chris Johnson

33. What is the purpose of this letter?

    (A) To recommend Ms. Burnett for the systems engineer position

    (B) To apologize to Ms. Burnett and her colleagues for an error

    (C) To introduce Chris Johnson to Ms. Burnett's co-workers

    (D) To thank Ms. Burnett for holding an interview

34. What is suggested about Mr. Johnson?

    (A) He lost interest in working for MET Microsystems.

    (B) He lacks experience in systems development.

    (C) He is confident that he is qualified for the post.

    (D) He has never seen Ms. Burnett and her associates.

35. If she chooses to, how will Ms. Burnett contact Mr. Johnson?

    (A) Write a letter

    (B) Get together in person

    (C) Send a fax

    (D) Call or e-mail

Sunny Hills Gym
Special Introductory Offer

Feeling like you are carrying around a bit of extra weight? Did you enjoy the holidays a bit too much? Have you been feeling more tired than usual recently? Come to Sunny Hills Gym and try our Refresh Program Special. During this month only, you can enjoy all the equipment and classes offered for the introductory price of $65. Bring a friend and the two of you can join for $100.

Program Pricing		
Sunrise	6 A.M. - 10 A.M.	**$40**
Day Tripper	10 A.M. - 6 P.M.	**$65**
Moonlight	6 P.M. - 11 P.M.	**$45**
Freedom	6 A.M. - 11 P.M.	**$95**
Full on Freedom	6 A.M. - 11 P.M.	**$125** (includes all classes)
Refresh Program Special	6 A.M. - 11 P.M.	**$65** ($100 for 2)
Classes		**$5** per session

*The above prices include 5% state tax.

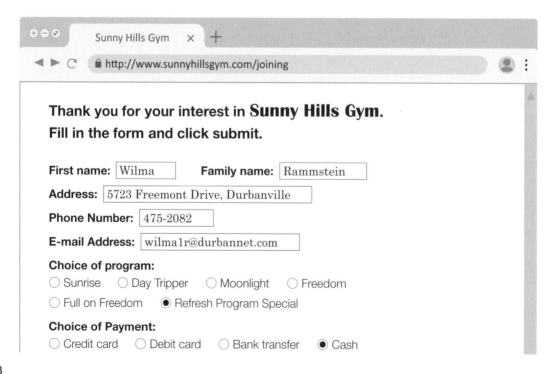

Sunny Hills Gym

http://www.sunnyhillsgym.com/joining

Thank you for your interest in Sunny Hills Gym.
Fill in the form and click submit.

First name: Wilma   Family name: Rammstein

Address: 5723 Freemont Drive, Durbanville

Phone Number: 475-2082

E-mail Address: wilma1r@durbannet.com

Choice of program:
○ Sunrise   ○ Day Tripper   ○ Moonlight   ○ Freedom
○ Full on Freedom   ● Refresh Program Special

Choice of Payment:
○ Credit card   ○ Debit card   ○ Bank transfer   ● Cash

Comments:

> I am joining the Refresh Program Special with my friend Ms. Drittler. We look forward to joining some classes on either Tuesday or Thursday afternoons.

CLICK HERE to go to the payment page.

An electronic copy of this document will be sent to your e-mail address. If you chose Cash as your payment option, please bring a copy of this form with you to the gym within seven days. To print a copy of this form, please **CLICK HERE**.

To:	wilma1r@durbannet.com
From:	joining@sunnyhillsgym.com
Subject:	Welcome to Sunny Hills Gym
Date:	September 8

Dear Ms. Rammstein,

Thank you for joining Sunny Hills Gym. We are pleased to welcome you and your friend, Ms. Drittler, to our group. We look forward to meeting you in person when you come to the gym. Please note that parking is available only behind the gym, not next to the building.

You mentioned that you are interested in joining classes on either Tuesday or Thursday afternoons. However, in case you want to join the classes in the mornings, we strongly recommend that you book in advance because they are very popular. Reservations can be made online from our webpage. It is also possible to join at the gym if there are any vacancies.

When you come the first day, you will need to bring a few things. Please do not forget to bring a copy of your registration and some identification to confirm your identity. You selected cash as your form of payment. We will need your payment at that time.

At the end of the program period we will ask you to complete a questionnaire.

Wishing you a warm welcome,
All the staff at Sunny Hills Gym

36. What is the purpose of the advertisement?

(A) To publicize a program valid for a limited period

(B) To introduce a new health insurance plan

(C) To promote exercise equipment

(D) To announce the grand opening of an affiliated gym

37. How much will Ms. Rammstein have to pay to join the gym?

(A) $50

(B) $65

(C) $100

(D) $125

38. In the e-mail, the phrase "in person" in paragraph 1, line 3, is closest in meaning to

(A) one by one

(B) arm in arm

(C) step by step

(D) face to face

39. What is Ms. Rammstein asked to do?

(A) Bring some identification

(B) Pay by bank transfer

(C) Avoid the morning classes

(D) Respond to the survey on the first day

40. What is NOT true about Sunny Hills Gym?

(A) All prices for programs and lessons include tax.

(B) Members cannot park their cars next to the gym.

(C) Members absolutely have to book classes beforehand.

(D) They accept not only credit cards but also debit cards.

Key Vocabulary

●衣食

□**1.** clothes, clothing, garment — 名 衣服、衣料品
    attire — 名 (特別な) 服装

□**2.** detergent — 名 洗剤

□**3.** fabric — 名 生地
    textile — 名 織物
    texture — 名 手触り

□**4.** fold — 動 ～を折りたたむ

□**5.** hang — 動 ～を吊るす

□**6.** laundry — 名 洗濯物、クリーニング店
    do the laundry — 句 洗濯する
    cleaner — 名 クリーニング店

□**7.** cookware — 名 調理器具
    tableware — 名 食器類

□**8.** cupboard — 名 食器棚

□**9.** dairy — 名 乳製品

□**10.** grocery store — 名 食料雑貨店

□**11.** microwave oven — 名 電子レンジ

□**12.** refrigerator, fridge — 名 冷蔵庫

□**13.** stove — 名 コンロ

□**14.** utensils — 名 台所用品

●住

□**15.** appliance — 名 電化製品、家電

□**16.** attach — 動 ～を取り付ける
    equip — 動 ～に備え付ける
    install — 動 ～を設置する

□**17.** ceiling — 名 天井

□**18.** comfortable — 形 居心地の良い、快適な

□**19.** condo(minium) — 名 分譲マンション

□**20.** drawer — 名 引き出し

□**21.** electricity — 名 電気

□**22.** enter — 動 ～に入る
    entrance — 名 入口
    exit — 名 出口

□**23.** equipment — 名 設備、装備

□**24.** furniture — 名 家具

□**25.** hardware store — 名 ホームセンター

□**26.** ladder — 名 はしご

□**27.** landlord — 名 家主
    tenant — 名 賃借人

□**28.** light fixture — 名 照明器具
    light bulb — 名 電球

□**29.** mow — 動 ～を刈る
    trim — 動 ～を刈り揃える

□**30.** overlook — 動 ～を見下ろす位置にある

□**31.** patio — 名 中庭

□**32.** plumber — 名 配管工

□**33.** property, real estate — 名 不動産

□**34.** remodel — 動 ～を改築する

□**35.** rent — 名 家賃 動 ～を賃貸する

□**36.** repair, fix — 動 ～を修理する

□**37.** replace — 動 ～を交換する

□**38.** resident — 名 居住者、住民

□**39.** stairs, staircase — 名 階段

□**40.** suburb — 名 郊外
    urban — 形 都会の

□**41.** turn on — 句 ～をつける
    turn off — 句 ～を消す

□**42.** utilities — 名 公共料金

□**43.** view — 名 眺め、視界

●その他

□**44.** blackout — 名 停電

□**45.** convenience — 名 便利さ
    convenient — 形 便利な

□**46.** evacuate — 動 ～を避難させる、避難する

□**47.** household — 名 形 世帯、家庭 (の)

□**48.** lean against — 句 ～に寄りかかる

□**49.** monthly — 形 毎月の
    weekly — 形 毎週の

□**50.** neighborhood — 名 近所
    nearby — 形 副 すぐ近くの (に)

UNIT 2 Shopping

☐ **1.**	additional fee, extra charge	名 追加手数料、追加料金
☐ **2.**	available	形 入手可能な、利用できる
☐ **3.**	bill	名 請求書、勘定書
	receipt	名 レシート、領収書
	statement	名 明細書
☐ **4.**	business days	名 営業日
	business hours	名 営業時間
☐ **5.**	cafeteria	名 セルフサービス式の食堂
	diner	名 小食堂、食事客
☐ **6.**	cashier	名 レジ係
	register	名 レジ
☐ **7.**	change	名 おつり
☐ **8.**	charge	名 手数料　動 ～を請求する
☐ **9.**	clerk, staff	名 店員
	sales representative	名 販売員
☐ **10.**	complain	動 苦情を言う
	complaint	名 苦情、クレーム
☐ **11.**	currently	副 現在は
☐ **12.**	customer	名 顧客
	shopper	名 買い物客
☐ **13.**	defect	名 欠陥
	defective product	名 欠陥品
☐ **14.**	deliver	動 ～を配達する
	delivery	名 配達
	overnight delivery	名 翌日配送
	by express	句 速達で
☐ **15.**	discount	名 動 (～を) 割引 (する)
☐ **16.**	display	名 動 (～を) 陳列 (する)
☐ **17.**	dozen	名 ダース、12個
☐ **18.**	estimate	名 見積り　動 ～を見積もる
☐ **19.**	exchange	名 動 (～を) 交換 (する)
☐ **20.**	expensive	形 高価な
☐ **21.**	feedback	名 感想、意見
	testimonial	名 お客様の声
	review	名 批評、評論
☐ **22.**	floor	名 階
☐ **23.**	fragile	形 壊れやすい
☐ **24.**	guarantee, warranty	名 保証
☐ **25.**	in advance, beforehand	副 前もって
☐ **26.**	inquire, ask	動 ～に問い合わせる、～に尋ねる
	inquiry	名 問合せ、質問
☐ **27.**	instruction	名 使用説明書
	specifications	名 仕様書
☐ **28.**	invoice	名 送り状
☐ **29.**	latest	形 名 最新の (もの)
☐ **30.**	launch, release	名 動 (～を) 発売 (する)
☐ **31.**	merchandise, goods, item	名 商品
☐ **32.**	out of stock	句 在庫切れで
	in stock	句 入荷して
	on back order	句 入荷待ちで
☐ **33.**	package, parcel	名 小包
☐ **34.**	patronage	名 愛顧、ひいき
☐ **35.**	pay	動 ～を支払う
	payment	名 支払い
☐ **36.**	place an order	句 注文する
☐ **37.**	popularity	名 人気
☐ **38.**	purchase, buy	動 ～を購入する、～を買う
☐ **39.**	quality	名 形 質、上質 (な)
	quantity	名 数量
☐ **40.**	questionnaire	名 アンケート用紙
☐ **41.**	reasonable, affordable	形 手頃な値段の
	inexpensive,	形 安価な、低価格の
	cheap	形 安い
☐ **42.**	refund	名 動 (～を) 返金 (する)
	reimburse	動 ～を返金する、～を払い戻す
☐ **43.**	return, take back	動 ～を返品する
☐ **44.**	shelf	名 棚
☐ **45.**	ship	動 ～を発送する
	shipment	名 発送
	dispatch, expedite	動 ～を急いで発送する
☐ **46.**	special offer	名 特別提供 (品)
☐ **47.**	sport gear	名 スポーツ用品
☐ **48.**	subscribe to	動 ～を定期購読する
	subscription	名 定期購読
☐ **49.**	up to	句 最大～まで
☐ **50.**	voucher	名 引換券
	coupon	名 割引券、クーポン

UNIT 3   Parties & Events

●パーティー

- ☐ **1.** anniversary   名 ～周年、記念日
- ☐ **2.** atmosphere   名 雰囲気
- ☐ **3.** attend   動 ～に出席する
  attendance   名 出席
  attendee   名 出席者
- ☐ **4.** banquet   名 宴会
- ☐ **5.** beverage   名 飲料
- ☐ **6.** casual, informal   形 カジュアルな、略式の
- ☐ **7.** catering   名 仕出し、ケータリング
- ☐ **8.** complimentary, free   形 無料の
- ☐ **9.** cuisine, dish, meal   名 料理
- ☐ **10.** hold   動 ～を開催する
  be held,   動 開催される
  take place
- ☐ **11.** participant   名 参加者
- ☐ **12.** participate in,   動 ～に参加する、加わる
  take part in,
  join
- ☐ **13.** prepare   動 ～を準備する
- ☐ **14.** reception   名 歓迎会、パーティー
  farewell party   名 送別会
- ☐ **15.** refreshments   名 軽い飲食物
- ☐ **16.** serve   動 ～を給仕する
- ☐ **17.** vegan   名 絶対菜食主義者、ヴィーガン

●イベント

- ☐ **18.** activity   名 活動
- ☐ **19.** actor   名 俳優
  actress   名 女優
- ☐ **20.** admission   名 入場（料）、入会（費）
- ☐ **21.** applaud   動 拍手する、～に拍手を送る
  applause   名 拍手
- ☐ **22.** author   名 著者
- ☐ **23.** award, prize   名 賞
- ☐ **24.** book, reserve   動 ～を予約する
  booking, reservation   名 予約
- ☐ **25.** box office   名 チケット売り場
- ☐ **26.** complex   名 複合施設
- ☐ **27.** critic   名 批評家、評論家
  review   名 動 （～を）論評（する）

- ☐ **28.** donate, contribute   動 ～を寄付する
  donation, contribution   名 寄付
- ☐ **29.** excellent   形 優秀な、素晴らしい
- ☐ **30.** exhibit   動 ～を展示する   名 展示品
  exhibition   名 展覧会
- ☐ **31.** feature   動 ～を目玉にする、～を特集する
- ☐ **32.** feedback   名 感想、意見
- ☐ **33.** fund   名 基金、資金
    動 ～に資金を提供する
  fund-raising   形 資金調達のための、慈善の
- ☐ **34.** generous   形 寛大な、気前の良い
  generosity   名 寛大さ、気前の良さ
- ☐ **35.** host   動 ～を主催する
- ☐ **36.** impressive   形 印象的な
  impression   名 印象
- ☐ **37.** keynote speech   名 基調講演
- ☐ **38.** organization   名 団体
- ☐ **39.** outdoor,   形 戸外の、野外の
  open-air
- ☐ **40.** performance   名 演奏、演技
- ☐ **41.** raise money   句 資金を集める
- ☐ **42.** register, enroll   動 ～を登録する
  registration, enrollment   名 登録
- ☐ **43.** renovate   動 ～を改装する
  renovation   名 改装
  restore   動 ～を修復する
  restoration   名 修復
- ☐ **44.** reputation   名 評判
- ☐ **45.** spectator, audience   名 観客、視聴者
- ☐ **46.** sponsor   名 スポンサー、出資者
    動 ～に資金援助する
- ☐ **47.** stadium   名 スタジアム
- ☐ **48.** theater   名 劇場
- ☐ **49.** upcoming   形 次回の、今度の
- ☐ **50.** venue   名 会場

UNIT
4 **Traffic & Travel**

● 交通

- □ **1.** area 名 地域
  region 名 区域
- □ **2.** available 形 利用できる、入手可能な
- □ **3.** board 動 ～に乗り込む
  get on 句 ～に乗る
  get off 句 ～を降りる
- □ **4.** commute 動 通勤する
- □ **5.** crosswalk 名 横断歩道
  intersection 名 交差点
- □ **6.** curb 名 縁石
  sidewalk, 名 歩道
  walkway
- □ **7.** downtown 名 形 繁華街 (の)
- □ **8.** express 名 形 急行 (の)
- □ **9.** fare 名 運賃、料金
- □ **10.** fine 名 罰金
- □ **11.** parking lot 名 駐車場
- □ **12.** pedestrian 名 歩行者
- □ **13.** proceed, head 動 進む、向かう
- □ **14.** sign 名 標識、看板
- □ **15.** make [take] a detour 句 迂回する
- □ **16.** transportation 名 輸送機関、乗物
- □ **17.** vehicle, 名 乗物、車
  automobile

● 旅行

- □ **18.** accommodate 動 ～を収容できる
  accommodation 名 宿泊 (設備)
  inn 名 ホテル
- □ **19.** aisle seat 名 通路側の席
  window seat 名 窓側の席
- □ **20.** arrival 名 到着
  departure 名 出発
- □ **21.** baggage, luggage 名 手荷物
- □ **22.** baggage claim (area) 名 手荷物受取所
- □ **23.** belongings 名 所持品
  valuables 名 貴重品
- □ **24.** book, reserve 動 ～を予約する
  booking, reservation 名 予約
- □ **25.** cancel, 動 ～を中止する
  call off

- □ **26.** check in 名 句 チェックイン (する)
  check out 名 句 チェックアウト (する)
- □ **27.** check-in counter 名 チェックインカウンター
- □ **28.** confirm 動 ～を確認する
  confirmation 名 確認
- □ **29.** connect 動 ～に接続する、～に連絡する
  connection 名 接続、連絡
- □ **30.** delay 名 動 (～を) 遅延 (させる)
- □ **31.** destination 名 目的地
- □ **32.** domestic flight 名 国内線
  international flight 名 国際線
- □ **33.** fasten 動 ～を締める、～を固定する
- □ **34.** flight attendant, 名 客室乗務員
  cabin attendant
- □ **35.** itinerary 名 旅程表
- □ **36.** landmark 名 目印 (となる建造物)、史跡
- □ **37.** local 形 現地の、地元の
- □ **38.** lost and found 名 遺失物取扱所
- □ **39.** package tour 名 パック旅行
- □ **40.** passenger 名 乗客
- □ **41.** postpone, 動 ～を延期する
  put off
- □ **42.** shuttle 名 定期往復便
- □ **43.** sightseeing 名 観光
- □ **44.** souvenir 名 記念品、土産
- □ **45.** take off 句 離陸する
  land 動 着陸する
- □ **46.** time table 名 時刻表
- □ **47.** travel agency 名 旅行代理店
- □ **48.** unfortunately 副 あいにく、残念ながら
- □ **49.** vacant 形 空いている
  vacancy 名 空室、空席
  occupied 形 使用中の
- □ **50.** via, by way of 前 ～経由で

☐ **1.**	accurate	形 正確な	
☐ **2.**	achieve	動 〜を達成する	
☐ **3.**	adjust	動 〜を調整する	
	reschedule	動 〜を再調整する、〜を延期する	
☐ **4.**	adopt	動 〜を採用する、〜を導入する	
☐ **5.**	apologize	動 謝罪する	
	apology	名 謝罪	
☐ **6.**	approximately	副 およそ、約	
☐ **7.**	arrange	動 〜を手配する	
☐ **8.**	attend a meeting	句 会議に出席する	
☐ **9.**	be in charge of	句 〜を担当して	
	be responsible for	句 〜に責任がある	
☐ **10.**	bulk order	名 一括注文、大口発注	
☐ **11.**	business days	名 営業日	
	business hours	名 営業時間	
☐ **12.**	clerk	名 事務員、店員	
☐ **13.**	colleague, coworker	名 同僚	
☐ **14.**	committee	名 委員会	
☐ **15.**	complain	動 苦情を言う	
	complaint	名 苦情、クレーム	
☐ **16.**	conclude	動 結論付ける	
	conclusion	名 結論	
☐ **17.**	confirm	動 〜を確かめる	
	confirmation	名 確認	
☐ **18.**	deadline	名 締め切り	
☐ **19.**	deal with, handle, process	句 動 〜を処理する	
☐ **20.**	document	名 文書	
☐ **21.**	effectively, efficiently	副 効率的に、効果的に	
☐ **22.**	enclose	動 〜を同封する	
☐ **23.**	encourage A to do	句 Aに〜するよう促す	
☐ **24.**	equipment	名 設備、備品	
	office supplies	名 事務用品	
	stationery	名 文房具	
☐ **25.**	extension	名 内線	
☐ **26.**	flexible	形 柔軟な、融通のきく	
☐ **27.**	hand in, submit	句 動 〜を提出する	
☐ **28.**	identification	名 身分証明書	
	identify	動 〜を特定する	
☐ **29.**	improve	動 〜を改善する	

☐ **30.**	incentive	名 報奨（金）	
		形 やる気を起こさせる	
☐ **31.**	in-house	形 副 社内の（で）	
	interoffice	形 社内の	
	memo(randum)	名 社内文書、回覧	
☐ **32.**	invoice	名 送り状	
☐ **33.**	management	名 管理、経営	
☐ **34.**	meeting, conference	名 会議	
	convention	名 総会	
☐ **35.**	notify, inform	動 〜に知らせる、〜に通知する	
	notification	名 通知（書）	
☐ **36.**	photocopier, copier	名 コピー機	
☐ **37.**	policy	名 方針	
☐ **38.**	presentation	名 プレゼン、発表	
☐ **39.**	priority	名 優先事項、優先順位	
☐ **40.**	receptionist	名 受付係	
	secretary	名 秘書	
☐ **41.**	require, call for	動 〜を要求する	
☐ **42.**	routine	名 決まりきった仕事	
☐ **43.**	sales quota	名 売上ノルマ	
☐ **44.**	sales representative, salesperson	名 営業担当者	
☐ **45.**	seminar, workshop	名 研究会、研修会	
☐ **46.**	solution	名 解決（策）	
☐ **47.**	specific	形 特定の、具体的な	
☐ **48.**	staple	動 〜をホチキスで留める	
	stapler	名 ホチキス	
☐ **49.**	subordinate	名 部下	
	supervisor, boss	名 上司	
☐ **50.**	work overtime	句 残業する	

UNIT 6 Marketing & ICT

● マーケティング

□ **1.** advertise 動 ～を広告する、～を宣伝する
advertisement 名 広告

□ **2.** affordable, 形 手ごろな値段の
reasonable

□ **3.** analyze 動 ～を分析する
analysis 名 分析

□ **4.** announce 動 ～を発表する、～を公表する
announcement 名 発表、公表

□ **5.** article 名 記事

□ **6.** attract 動 ～を引き付ける、～を魅惑する
attractive 形 魅力的な

□ **7.** broadcast, air 名 動 (～を) 放送 (する)

□ **8.** brochure 名 パンフレット、小冊子

□ **9.** commercial 形 商業の 名 コマーシャル

□ **10.** consume 動 ～を消費する
consumer 名 消費者

□ **11.** copyright 名 著作権

□ **12.** cover 動 ～を報道する
coverage 名 報道

□ **13.** customer satisfaction 名 顧客満足 (度)

□ **14.** feedback 名 反応、意見
testimonial 名 お客様の声

□ **15.** flyer, leaflet 名 チラシ

□ **16.** impressive 形 印象的な

□ **17.** improve 動 ～を改善する

□ **18.** influence 名 動 (～に) 影響 (を及ぼす)
influential 形 影響力のある

□ **19.** issue 名 動 (～を) 発行 (する)

□ **20.** launch, release 名 動 (～を) 発売 [開始] (する)

□ **21.** marketing 名 マーケティング

□ **22.** outstanding 形 目立つ、優れた

□ **23.** persuasive 形 説得力のある
confident 形 自信のある

□ **24.** press conference 名 記者会見

□ **25.** promotion campaign 名 販促キャンペーン

□ **26.** public relations 名 広報活動、PR

□ **27.** publish 動 ～を出版する
publisher 名 出版社

□ **28.** questionnaire 名 アンケート用紙
conduct a survey 句 アンケート調査を行う

□ **29.** recommend 動 ～を推薦する、～を勧める

□ **30.** spokesperson 名 広報担当者

□ **31.** stress 動 ～を強調する

□ **32.** various 形 様々な

● 情報通信技術

□ **33.** access 名 アクセス
動 ～に接続する

□ **34.** application 名 アプリ
software 名 ソフトウエア

□ **35.** attach 動 ～を添付する

□ **36.** browse 動 ～を閲覧する、～を検索する
browser 名 ブラウザー (閲覧ソフト)

□ **37.** cellphone, 名 携帯電話
mobile phone
smart phone 名 スマートフォン

□ **38.** enter, 動 ～を入力する
input

□ **39.** function 名 機能

□ **40.** install 動 ～をインストールする

□ **41.** laptop 名 形 ノートパソコン (の)

□ **42.** manual 名 手引書、説明書

□ **43.** online 形 副 オンラインの (で)

□ **44.** recognition 名 認識
resolution 名 解像度

□ **45.** reply 名 動 返信 (する)
forward 動 ～を転送する

□ **46.** save 動 ～を保存する

□ **47.** sign up 句 サインアップ (加入) する

□ **48.** troubleshooting 名 形 トラブル解決 (の)、修理 (の)

□ **49.** update 名 動 (～を) アップデート (する)、更新 (する)

□ **50.** up-to-date, 形 最新式の、最先端の
cutting-edge,
state-of-the-art

●製造

☐ **1.** architect　　　名 建築家、設計者
　　architecture　　名 建築

☐ **2.** artificial　　　形 人工的な
　　synthetic　　　形 合成の

☐ **3.** assembly line　名 組み立てライン

☐ **4.** blueprint　　　名 設計図

☐ **5.** capacity　　　名 生産能力

☐ **6.** caution　　　　名 注意

☐ **7.** component　　名 部品

☐ **8.** construction　名 建設、建築工事

☐ **9.** develop　　　　動 ～を開発する
　　development　　名 開発
　　developer　　　名 開発業者

☐ **10.** dispose　　　　動 ～を処理する
　　disposal　　　　名 処理

☐ **11.** durable　　　　形 耐久性がある
　　durability　　　名 耐久性

☐ **12.** engineering　　名 工学（技術）

☐ **13.** experiment　　名 動 実験（する）

☐ **14.** facility　　　　名 設備、施設
　　plant, factory　名 工場

☐ **15.** garage　　　　名 車庫、自動車修理 [整備] 工場

☐ **16.** industrial waste　名 産業ごみ

☐ **17.** innovative　　　形 革新的な

☐ **18.** inspect　　　　動 ～を検査する、～を点検する
　　inspection　　　名 検査、点検

☐ **19.** instrument　　名 器具

☐ **20.** investigate　　動 (～を)調査する、(～を)研究する

☐ **21.** laboratory　　名 実験室、研究室

☐ **22.** maintenance　名 整備、メンテナンス

☐ **23.** manufacture　名 動 (～を)製造(する)
　　manufacturer　名 製造業者、メーカー

☐ **24.** material　　　　名 材料

☐ **25.** monitor　　　　動 ～を監視する

☐ **26.** operate　　　　動 ～を操作する
　　operation　　　名 操作、運転

☐ **27.** patent　　　　名 形 特許（の）

☐ **28.** produce　　　　動 ～を生産する、～を製造する
　　　　　　　　　　名 農産物

☐ **29.** product　　　　名 製品
　　production　　　名 生産、製造
　　productivity　　名 生産性

☐ **30.** prototype　　　名 試作品

☐ **31.** quality control　名 品質管理

☐ **32.** research　　　　名 動 (～を)研究(する)
　　R&D　　　　　　名 研究開発（部門）
　　(research and development)

☐ **33.** safety standard　名 安全基準

☐ **34.** supervisor　　　名 管理者、監督者

●物流

☐ **35.** cargo　　　　名 積荷、貨物
　　freight　　　　名 貨物運送

☐ **36.** container　　　名 貨物用コンテナ

☐ **37.** courier　　　　名 配達業者
　　carrier　　　　名 配達員

☐ **38.** distribution　　名 流通

☐ **39.** dock　　　　　名 埠頭
　　harbor　　　　名 港

☐ **40.** import　　　　名 動 (～を)輸入(する)
　　export　　　　名 動 (～を)輸出(する)

☐ **41.** inventory, stock　名 在庫

☐ **42.** load　　　　　名 積荷　動 ～を積み込む

☐ **43.** logistics　　　名 物流

☐ **44.** pile, stack　　動 ～を積み上げる

☐ **45.** prompt　　　　形 迅速な
　　promptly　　　副 迅速に

☐ **46.** provide,
　　supply　　　　動 ～を供給する
　　provider,
　　supplier　　　　名 供給業者

☐ **47.** retail　　　　名 小売り
　　retailer　　　　名 小売業者
　　wholesale　　　名 卸売り
　　wholesaler　　　名 卸売業者

☐ **48.** ship　　　　　動 ～を出荷する、～を発送する
　　shipment　　　名 出荷、発送
　　dispatch　　　動 ～を発送する

☐ **49.** vessel　　　　名 船舶

☐ **50.** warehouse, storage　名 倉庫

UNIT 8 Employment

- ☐ **1.** ability, capability 名 能力
- ☐ **2.** application (form) 名 応募用紙
- ☐ **3.** apply for 句 ～に申し込む / applicant 名 応募者
- ☐ **4.** appreciate 動 ～に感謝する
- ☐ **5.** attach 動 ～を添付する / enclose 動 ～を同封する
- ☐ **6.** background 名 経歴 / academic background 名 学歴
- ☐ **7.** business trip, extensive travel 名 出張
- ☐ **8.** candidate 名 候補者、志望者
- ☐ **9.** career, professional background 名 経歴
- ☐ **10.** confident 形 自信のある
- ☐ **11.** cover letter 名 カバーレター、添え状
- ☐ **12.** current, present 形 現在の / currently 副 現在
- ☐ **13.** decline 動 丁寧に断る
- ☐ **14.** degree 名 学位 / master's degree, MA 名 修士号
- ☐ **15.** desirable 形 望ましい / preferable 形 好ましい
- ☐ **16.** editor 名 編集者 / proofreader 名 校正者
- ☐ **17.** employ, hire 動 ～を雇用する / fire, dismiss 動 ～を解雇する
- ☐ **18.** employee 名 従業員 / employer 名 雇い主
- ☐ **19.** employment, hiring 名 雇用、採用
- ☐ **20.** enthusiastic 形 熱心な
- ☐ **21.** experience 名 動 (～を) 経験 (する) / experienced 形 経験豊富な
- ☐ **22.** fill out [in] 句 ～に記入する
- ☐ **23.** fluent 形 流ちょうな
- ☐ **24.** full-time 形 常勤の / permanent 形 常任の / part-time 形 非常勤の / temporary 形 臨時の
- ☐ **25.** graduate from 句 ～を卒業する
- ☐ **26.** industry 名 業界、産業
- ☐ **27.** interview 名 動 面接 (する)
- ☐ **28.** job fair 名 就職説明会
- ☐ **29.** job hunting, job searching 名 就職活動
- ☐ **30.** job opening, vacancy 名 空きポスト、欠員
- ☐ **31.** knowledge 名 知識
- ☐ **32.** major 名 形 動 専攻 (の、する)
- ☐ **33.** management 名 経営陣
- ☐ **34.** occupation 名 職業、職 / profession 名 専門職
- ☐ **35.** opportunity 名 機会
- ☐ **36.** orientation 名 新入社員向け説明会
- ☐ **37.** portfolio 名 作品集
- ☐ **38.** position 名 地位、職
- ☐ **39.** post 動 ～を掲載する 名 職
- ☐ **40.** practical 形 実務の
- ☐ **41.** qualified 形 資格のある / qualification 名 資格 / certificate 名 認定書
- ☐ **42.** receive 動 ～を受け取る
- ☐ **43.** recommend 動 ～を推薦する / recommendation 名 推薦 (状)
- ☐ **44.** recruit 動 ～を募集する、～を採用する 名 新入社員
- ☐ **45.** reference 名 照会先
- ☐ **46.** requirement 名 必要条件、要件
- ☐ **47.** respond 動 返事をする / response 名 返答、返事
- ☐ **48.** résumé, CV (curriculum vitae) 名 履歴書
- ☐ **49.** salary, paycheck 名 給料、給与 / wage 名 賃金 / commission 名 歩合
- ☐ **50.** welfare, benefits 名 福利厚生

- [ ] **1.** CEO
(chief executive officer) 名 最高経営責任者
- [ ] **2.** accept 動 ～を引き受ける、～を受け入れる
- [ ] **3.** allowance 名 手当
- [ ] **4.** as of,
effective from 句 ～付けで
- [ ] **5.** assign 動 ～を割り当てる
- [ ] **6.** be committed to 句 ～に熱心に取り組む
- [ ] **7.** be devoted to,
be dedicated to 句 ～に尽力する
- [ ] **8.** be eligible for,
be entitled to 句 ～の資格がある
- [ ] **9.** be in charge of 句 ～を担当して
- [ ] **10.** board of directors 名 取締役会、重役会
- [ ] **11.** branch
headquarters,
head office 名 支社、支店
名 本社、本店
- [ ] **12.** candidate 名 候補者
- [ ] **13.** chair(person) 名 議長
- [ ] **14.** clerical 形 事務の
- [ ] **15.** colleague,
coworker 名 同僚
- [ ] **16.** competent,
efficient 形 有能な
- [ ] **17.** confidential 形 秘密の、部外秘の
- [ ] **18.** consent to 動 ～に同意する
- [ ] **19.** contribute
contribution 動 貢献する
名 貢献
- [ ] **20.** department, division 名 部（門）
section 名 課
- [ ] **21.** designate
appoint,
assign 動 ～を指名［任命］する
動 ～を任命する
- [ ] **22.** diligent 形 勤勉な
- [ ] **23.** endeavor 名 努力
- [ ] **24.** evaluate
evaluation 動 ～を評価する
名 評価
- [ ] **25.** executive
director 名 幹部、重役
名 取締役、重役
- [ ] **26.** human resources (HR),
personnel 名 人事
- [ ] **27.** income 名 収入
- [ ] **28.** manager 名 部長
- [ ] **29.** orientation 名 新入社員向け説明会
- [ ] **30.** outstanding 形 抜きんでている
- [ ] **31.** paycheck 名 給与
- [ ] **32.** performance 名 業績
- [ ] **33.** persuade,
convince 動 ～を説得する
- [ ] **34.** previous, former 形 前の
- [ ] **35.** promising 形 前途有望な
- [ ] **36.** promote
promotion 動 ～を昇進させる
名 昇進
- [ ] **37.** proper,
appropriate,
suitable 形 適切な
- [ ] **38.** reception
farewell party 名 歓迎会、パーティー
名 送別会
- [ ] **39.** replace 動 ～の後任になる
- [ ] **40.** resign, quit
resignation 動 ～を辞職する、～を辞任する
名 辞職、辞任
- [ ] **41.** retire 動 定年退職する
- [ ] **42.** subordinate 名 部下
- [ ] **43.** subsidiary 名 系列子会社
- [ ] **44.** supervisor,
boss 名 上司
- [ ] **45.** take over 句 ～を引き継ぐ
- [ ] **46.** train
training session 動 ～を養成する、～を教育する
名 研修（期間）
- [ ] **47.** transfer,
relocate 動 ～を転勤させる、～を異動させる
- [ ] **48.** unexpectedly 副 予想外に、思いがけず
- [ ] **49.** vice president 名 副社長
- [ ] **50.** workplace 名 職場

□**1.**	abandon	動 ～を諦める、～を断念する
□**2.**	accept	動 ～を受け入れる、～を受諾する
	agree	動 同意する
□**3.**	advantage	名 有利な点、強み
	take advantage of	句 ～を利用する
□**4.**	agenda	名 議題
□**5.**	announce	動 ～を発表する、～を公表する
	announcement	名 発表、公表
□**6.**	annual	名 年次の、年に一回の
□**7.**	attorney, lawyer	名 弁護士
□**8.**	boost	動 ～を伸ばす、～を増やす
	rise	動 上がる
	skyrocket, soar	動 急騰する
□**9.**	budget	名 予算（案）
□**10.**	client	名 顧客、取引先
□**11.**	collaborate	動 共同研究する、協力する
	collaboration	名 共同研究、協力
□**12.**	competitor	名 競争相手
	competition	名 競争（相手）
	competitive	形 競争力のある、競争の激しい
□**13.**	compromise	名 動 妥協（する）
□**14.**	consult	動 （～に）相談する
	consultant	名 顧問、コンサルタント
□**15.**	consume	動 ～を消費する
	consumer	名 消費者
	consumption	名 消費
□**16.**	contract	名 動 契約（する）
□**17.**	deal	名 取引、契約　動 取り扱う
□**18.**	decade	名 10年（間）
□**19.**	decline	動 衰退する
	deteriorate	動 悪化する
□**20.**	demand	名 需要　動 ～を要求する
	supply	名 動 （～を）供給（する）
□**21.**	depression	名 長期的不景気
	recession	名 一時的景気後退
□**22.**	effect	名 効果
	effective	形 効果的な
□**23.**	entrepreneur	名 企業家、起業家
□**24.**	expand, enlarge	動 ～を拡大する
	downsize	動 ～を縮小する
□**25.**	expect, anticipate	動 ～を予想する
□**26.**	explain, describe, account for	動 ～を説明する

□**27.**	firm, company, business, corporation, enterprise	名 会社、企業
□**28.**	found, establish	動 ～を設立する
□**29.**	increase	名 動 増加（する、させる）
	decrease,	名 動 減少（する、させる）
	reduce	動 ～を減少させる
□**30.**	institution	名 制度、機関
□**31.**	launch	名 動 （～を）開始［発売］する
□**32.**	merger, M&A (merger and acquisition)	名 合併買収
□**33.**	negotiate	動 交渉する
	negotiation	名 交渉
□**34.**	outsource	動 ～を外注する
□**35.**	partner up	句 提携する
	business partnership, business alliance	名 業務提携
□**36.**	potential customer	名 潜在的な客
	prospective customer	名 見込み客
□**37.**	predict, foresee	動 ～を予測する
□**38.**	profit	名 利益
	profitable	形 儲かる
	loss	名 損失
□**39.**	propose	動 ～を提案する
	proposal, suggestion	名 提案
□**40.**	prospect, outlook	名 見通し
□**41.**	prosperous	形 繁盛している
□**42.**	regulation	名 規制
	deregulation	名 規制緩和
□**43.**	second quarter	名 第2四半期
□**44.**	sign	動 ～に署名する
	signature	名 署名、調印
□**45.**	stockholder, shareholder	名 株主
□**46.**	strategy	名 戦略
□**47.**	streamline, simplify	動 ～を簡素化する
□**48.**	target	名 対象、達成目標
□**49.**	transfer, relocate	動 ～を移転させる
□**50.**	vision	名 構想

UNIT 11 Health & Environment

●健康

- ☐ **1.** ambulance 名 救急車
- ☐ **2.** benefit, allowance 名 手当、給付
- ☐ **3.** checkup 名 健康診断
- ☐ **4.** cover 動 ～を保障する
  coverage 名 保障 (額)
- ☐ **5.** cure, treatment 名 治療
- ☐ **6.** dentist 名 歯科医
- ☐ **7.** disease, illness 名 病気
- ☐ **8.** flu 名 インフルエンザ
  cold 名 風邪
- ☐ **9.** headache 名 頭痛
  toothache 名 歯痛
- ☐ **10.** health insurance 名 健康保険
- ☐ **11.** medicine, drug 名 内服薬
- ☐ **12.** patient 名 患者
  形 忍耐強い
- ☐ **13.** pharmacy 名 薬局
  pharmaceutical 形 製薬の
- ☐ **14.** physician 名 内科医
  surgeon 名 外科医
- ☐ **15.** prescribe 動 ～を処方する
  prescription 名 処方箋
- ☐ **16.** prevent 動 ～を予防する
- ☐ **17.** recover 動 回復する
  recovery 名 回復
- ☐ **18.** sick leave 名 病気休暇
  paid leave [vacation] 名 有給休暇
- ☐ **19.** side effect 名 副作用
- ☐ **20.** suffer from, 句 ～を患う
  come down with
- ☐ **21.** symptom 名 症状
- ☐ **22.** urgent 形 緊急の
  emergency 名 救急
- ☐ **23.** welfare, 名 福利厚生、福祉
  benefits

●環境

- ☐ **24.** alternative 名 形 代替 (の)
- ☐ **25.** approval 名 賛成
- ☐ **26.** atmosphere 名 大気、空気
- ☐ **27.** authorities 名 当局
- ☐ **28.** carbon dioxide 名 二酸化炭素
- ☐ **29.** city council 名 市議会
- ☐ **30.** community 名 地域社会
- ☐ **31.** county 名 郡
  state 名 (米国などの) 州
- ☐ **32.** eco-friendly, 形 環境に優しい
  environmentally friendly
  sustainable 形 持続可能な、環境に優しい
- ☐ **33.** eliminate, remove 動 ～を除去する
- ☐ **34.** emit 動 ～を排出する
  emission 名 排出
- ☐ **35.** environment 名 環境
- ☐ **36.** fuel 名 燃料
  resource 名 資源
- ☐ **37.** garbage, waste, 名 ごみ
  trash
- ☐ **38.** mayor 名 市長
  governor 名 知事
- ☐ **39.** municipal 形 地方自治の
- ☐ **40.** oppose, 動 ～に反対する
  object to,
  be against
- ☐ **41.** opposition 名 反対
- ☐ **42.** pollute, contaminate 動 ～を汚染する
  pollution, contamination 名 汚染、公害
- ☐ **43.** protect, 動 ～を保護する
  preserve
- ☐ **44.** protest 動 ～に抗議する
- ☐ **45.** refuse, reject, 動 ～を拒否する
  turn down
- ☐ **46.** resident 名 住民、居住者
- ☐ **47.** reusable, 形 再利用可能な
  renewable
- ☐ **48.** solar energy 名 太陽光エネルギー
- ☐ **49.** support, 動 ～に賛成する
  agree with,
  approve of,
  be for,
  be in favor of
- ☐ **50.** toxic 形 有毒な

☐ **1.** CFO (chief financial officer) 名 最高財務責任者

☐ **2.** account 名 銀行口座

☐ **3.** accountant 名 会計士、会計係

☐ **4.** accurate 形 正確な

☐ **5.** annual 形 毎年の、年一回の

☐ **6.** assess 動 ～を評価する、～を査定する

☐ **7.** asset 名 資産

☐ **8.** audit 名 監査

☐ **9.** bankruptcy 名 破産、倒産

☐ **10.** budget 名 予算

☐ **11.** calculate 動 ～を計算する / calculation 名 計算

☐ **12.** capital 名 資本

☐ **13.** check 名 小切手

☐ **14.** check the balance 句 残額を調べる

☐ **15.** compensate 動 賠償する / compensation 名 賠償（金）

☐ **16.** cost, expense, expenditure 名 経費、費用

☐ **17.** debt, liabilities 名 負債、債務

☐ **18.** deposit 動 ～を預ける 名 手付金、内金

☐ **19.** due 形 支払期日の来た、/ overdue 形 期限が過ぎた、滞納の

☐ **20.** exchange 動 ～を両替する 名 取引所、為替

☐ **21.** exhaust 動 ～を使い果たす

☐ **22.** expire 動 期限が切れる、失効する

☐ **23.** figure 名 数字、図

☐ **24.** finance 名 財務、金融 動 ～に融資する / financial 形 財務の、金融の

☐ **25.** fiscal year (FY) 名 事業年度

☐ **26.** fund 名 基金 動 ～に資金提供する

☐ **27.** gradually 副 徐々に

☐ **28.** in a row 句 連続して

☐ **29.** interest 名 利子、利息

☐ **30.** invest 動 ～を投資する / investment 名 投資

☐ **31.** loan 名 融資 動 ～に…を貸す / mortgage 名 住宅ローン

☐ **32.** optimistic 形 楽観的な

☐ **33.** outstanding 形 未払いの

☐ **34.** procedure 名 手続き

☐ **35.** prospect, outlook 名 見通し

☐ **36.** quarter 名 四半期

☐ **37.** reliable 形 信頼できる

☐ **38.** reminder 名 督促状

☐ **39.** revenue 名 収益、収入

☐ **40.** revise 動 ～を修正する

☐ **41.** save 動 貯金する / savings 名 貯蓄

☐ **42.** specific 形 特定の、具体的な

☐ **43.** stable, steady 形 安定した

☐ **44.** stock market 名 株式市場

☐ **45.** surpass 動 ～を上回る

☐ **46.** tax 名 税金

☐ **47.** teller 名 銀行の窓口係 / bank clerk 名 銀行員

☐ **48.** transfer 動 ～を振り込む / remit 動 ～を送金する

☐ **49.** valid 形 有効な

☐ **50.** withdraw 動 ～を引き出す

このシールをはがすと
CheckLink 利用のための
「教科書固有番号」が
記載されています。

一度はがすと元に戻すことは
できませんのでご注意下さい。

◀ここからはがして下さい

4110 SEIZE THE KEYS
(TOEIC)

本書にはCD（別売）があります

SEIZE THE KEYS OF THE TOEIC® L&R TEST

TOEIC® L&Rテスト攻略の鍵

2020年1月20日　初版第1刷発行
2024年2月20日　初版第6刷発行

著　者　　安　丸　雅　子
　　　　　渡　邉　晶　子
　　　　　砂　川　典　子
　　　　　高　森　暁　子
　　　　　十　時　　　康
　　　　　Andrew Zitzmann

発行者　　福　岡　正　人
発行所　　株式会社　金星堂

（〒101-0051）東京都千代田区神田神保町 3-21
　　　　Tel　（03）3263-3828（営業部）
　　　　　　　（03）3263-3997（編集部）
　　　　Fax　（03）3263-0716
　　　　http://www.kinsei-do.co.jp

編集担当　池田恭子・松本明子　　　　　　Printed in Japan
印刷所・製本所／倉敷印刷株式会社

ISBN978-4-7647-4110-2　C1082

Review Test 1 マークシート

学籍番号	
ふりがな	
名　前	

LISTENING SECTION

Part 1

No.	ANSWER A B C D
1	Ⓐ Ⓑ Ⓒ Ⓓ
2	Ⓐ Ⓑ Ⓒ Ⓓ

Part 2

No.	ANSWER A B C
3	Ⓐ Ⓑ Ⓒ
4	Ⓐ Ⓑ Ⓒ
5	Ⓐ Ⓑ Ⓒ
6	Ⓐ Ⓑ Ⓒ

No.	ANSWER A B C
7	Ⓐ Ⓑ Ⓒ
8	Ⓐ Ⓑ Ⓒ

Part 3

No.	ANSWER A B C D
9	Ⓐ Ⓑ Ⓒ Ⓓ
10	Ⓐ Ⓑ Ⓒ Ⓓ
11	Ⓐ Ⓑ Ⓒ Ⓓ
12	Ⓐ Ⓑ Ⓒ Ⓓ

No.	ANSWER A B C D
13	Ⓐ Ⓑ Ⓒ Ⓓ
14	Ⓐ Ⓑ Ⓒ Ⓓ

Part 4

No.	ANSWER A B C D
15	Ⓐ Ⓑ Ⓒ Ⓓ
16	Ⓐ Ⓑ Ⓒ Ⓓ
17	Ⓐ Ⓑ Ⓒ Ⓓ
18	Ⓐ Ⓑ Ⓒ Ⓓ

No.	ANSWER A B C D
19	Ⓐ Ⓑ Ⓒ Ⓓ
20	Ⓐ Ⓑ Ⓒ Ⓓ

READING SECTION

Part 5

No.	ANSWER A B C D
21	Ⓐ Ⓑ Ⓒ Ⓓ
22	Ⓐ Ⓑ Ⓒ Ⓓ
23	Ⓐ Ⓑ Ⓒ Ⓓ
24	Ⓐ Ⓑ Ⓒ Ⓓ

Part 6

No.	ANSWER A B C D
25	Ⓐ Ⓑ Ⓒ Ⓓ
26	Ⓐ Ⓑ Ⓒ Ⓓ
27	Ⓐ Ⓑ Ⓒ Ⓓ
28	Ⓐ Ⓑ Ⓒ Ⓓ

No.	ANSWER A B C D
29	Ⓐ Ⓑ Ⓒ Ⓓ
30	Ⓐ Ⓑ Ⓒ Ⓓ
31	Ⓐ Ⓑ Ⓒ Ⓓ
32	Ⓐ Ⓑ Ⓒ Ⓓ

Part 7

No.	ANSWER A B C D
33	Ⓐ Ⓑ Ⓒ Ⓓ
34	Ⓐ Ⓑ Ⓒ Ⓓ
35	Ⓐ Ⓑ Ⓒ Ⓓ
36	Ⓐ Ⓑ Ⓒ Ⓓ

No.	ANSWER A B C D
37	Ⓐ Ⓑ Ⓒ Ⓓ
38	Ⓐ Ⓑ Ⓒ Ⓓ
39	Ⓐ Ⓑ Ⓒ Ⓓ
40	Ⓐ Ⓑ Ⓒ Ⓓ

Review Test 2 マークシート

学籍番号	
ふりがな	
名　前	

LISTENING SECTION

Part 1

No.	ANSWER A B C D
1	Ⓐ Ⓑ Ⓒ Ⓓ
2	Ⓐ Ⓑ Ⓒ Ⓓ

Part 2

No.	ANSWER A B C
3	Ⓐ Ⓑ Ⓒ
4	Ⓐ Ⓑ Ⓒ
5	Ⓐ Ⓑ Ⓒ
6	Ⓐ Ⓑ Ⓒ

No.	ANSWER A B C
7	Ⓐ Ⓑ Ⓒ
8	Ⓐ Ⓑ Ⓒ

Part 3

No.	ANSWER A B C D
9	Ⓐ Ⓑ Ⓒ Ⓓ
10	Ⓐ Ⓑ Ⓒ Ⓓ
11	Ⓐ Ⓑ Ⓒ Ⓓ
12	Ⓐ Ⓑ Ⓒ Ⓓ

No.	ANSWER A B C D
13	Ⓐ Ⓑ Ⓒ Ⓓ
14	Ⓐ Ⓑ Ⓒ Ⓓ

Part 4

No.	ANSWER A B C D
15	Ⓐ Ⓑ Ⓒ Ⓓ
16	Ⓐ Ⓑ Ⓒ Ⓓ
17	Ⓐ Ⓑ Ⓒ Ⓓ
18	Ⓐ Ⓑ Ⓒ Ⓓ

No.	ANSWER A B C D
19	Ⓐ Ⓑ Ⓒ Ⓓ
20	Ⓐ Ⓑ Ⓒ Ⓓ

READING SECTION

Part 5

No.	ANSWER A B C D
21	Ⓐ Ⓑ Ⓒ Ⓓ
22	Ⓐ Ⓑ Ⓒ Ⓓ
23	Ⓐ Ⓑ Ⓒ Ⓓ
24	Ⓐ Ⓑ Ⓒ Ⓓ

Part 6

No.	ANSWER A B C D
25	Ⓐ Ⓑ Ⓒ Ⓓ
26	Ⓐ Ⓑ Ⓒ Ⓓ
27	Ⓐ Ⓑ Ⓒ Ⓓ
28	Ⓐ Ⓑ Ⓒ Ⓓ

No.	ANSWER A B C D
29	Ⓐ Ⓑ Ⓒ Ⓓ
30	Ⓐ Ⓑ Ⓒ Ⓓ
31	Ⓐ Ⓑ Ⓒ Ⓓ
32	Ⓐ Ⓑ Ⓒ Ⓓ

Part 7

No.	ANSWER A B C D
33	Ⓐ Ⓑ Ⓒ Ⓓ
34	Ⓐ Ⓑ Ⓒ Ⓓ
35	Ⓐ Ⓑ Ⓒ Ⓓ
36	Ⓐ Ⓑ Ⓒ Ⓓ

No.	ANSWER A B C D
37	Ⓐ Ⓑ Ⓒ Ⓓ
38	Ⓐ Ⓑ Ⓒ Ⓓ
39	Ⓐ Ⓑ Ⓒ Ⓓ
40	Ⓐ Ⓑ Ⓒ Ⓓ